The only existing photo of Bob's mother, Naomi Brown Beamon, taken just a few months before her death. She is holding Bob.

(Photo: Allsport/Tony Duffy.)

Mexico City, October 18, 1968. The Olympic Games. Photographer Tony Duffy captures Bob in mid-flight during his record breaking jump.

Bob in 1997 with his '68 Olympic teammate Ralph Boston

Bob's daughter, Deanna Taylor Beamon, age 14, with her 1st prize steer.

Bob and Milana, 1997.

THE MAN WHO COULD FLY

The Bob Beamon Story

Genesis Press, Inc.
315 Third Avenue North
Columbus, Mississippi 39701

The Man Who Could Fly: The Bob Beamon Story

ISBN 1-885478-89-5

Printed in the United States of America

FIRST EDITION

Book Design by Mary Beth Vickers

To David & Mark,
Dare to dream!
Enjoy the ride:
Milana Walter Beamon
2000

THE MAN WHO COULD FLY

The Bob Beamon Story

BOB BEAMON
and Milana Walter Beamon

Dedication

This book is dedicated to the loving memories of Naomi Brown Beamon, Bob's mother, and Willis Wilson Walter, Sr., Milana's father

Foreword

Milana and I have been working on telling the story of my life for two years now. It began as a film project and now has resulted in the book you are holding.

I learned about my life through living it. I had nothing to compare anything to. My childhood and adolescence was marked by a limited value system, no boundaries, and a "them and us" worldview. I was clueless.

After the 1968 Olympics I found myself thrust into a life of international celebrity, people with agendas, savvy dealmakers, emotional con artists, exposure to opportunities and places I hadn't even imagined. I was an athlete and a product of poverty, and I was wholly unprepared for the life forced upon me by my record-breaking jump.

But I believe someone was looking out for me. When I was growing up I saw guys my age dropping like flies from drug overdoses, bullets, or being sent away to prison. I remember saying to myself that I did not want to be like them. Yet, they were my role models, if only briefly. But it was being involved in sports that gave me another perspective on life and living, however subtle.

As an athlete, I was in the beginning undisciplined with a lot of raw talent. But raw talent does not make one a champion. That takes raw talent refined and combined with heart, hard work, and discipline. Through the encouragement I received from "the boys" and my coaches, and the inspiration I got from that feeling of winning, I was able to focus myself, hone my talent, make myself into a champion.

My personal life was another story. As a young man, I had a blind faith in the only person who seemed to love me. I was clueless about women. I was clueless when it came to the business side of sports. I didn't know how to be a celebrity. No matter how famous I became, I still clung to the familiar—and the familiar was hardly ever good for me.

Making mistakes is a part of living, there's just no way to get around that. I made many mistakes. I made some good choices. It takes courage and wisdom to make the right choices. Many times you don't get it right the first time, so you have to keep trying until you do. You have to keep going 'til you get it right. That one sentence sums up my story.

Now that this book is about to be a reality, I would like to express my gratitude to my mother, the late Naomi Brown Beamon, for watching over me; my grandmother, the late Bessie Beamon, for keeping her word to my mother; my uncle, the late Wilbert Brown; and all my maternal family, especially my cousin Diane Brown Brisbane for her compassion and love, and Aunt Emmie King for her love; the late Larry Ellis for being a father-figure; and the late James Beamon who finally turned his life around.

A special wish for my sister Nanette, and my brother Chris: May life become more like heaven and less like hell for you.

This book was written for one reason: To inspire you, the reader, to listen to your inner-self and not to outside influences. To understand that people can and do change, that patterns can be broken, and good things can happen to us all.

Finally, my heartfelt thanks to my wife, Milana Walter Beamon. This book would not have been possible, and my story never told, without her love and skill.

Bob Beamon
Miami, Florida
January 11, 1999

Introduction

When I returned to Miami from the Centennial Olympic Games in Atlanta in August 1996, I understood.

Bob had been nudging me about pursuing a film project about his life. I had filed it away in my mind. Atlanta was my first Olympic Games experience and my first Bob Beamon experience at the Olympic Games.

I still don't remember where I was or what I was doing on October 18, 1968, the day of his famous long jump of 29' 2 1/2". But destiny would make it one of the important dates in my life, as well.

What I witnessed in Atlanta was enormous admiration and respect for Bob, the champion, and for Bob, the man. He was honored during the opening ceremonies as one of ten "gold medal Olympic heroes that represent the achievements of all Olympians over the past one hundred years." As he walked to center stage in front of a combined stadium audience and television audience of over three billion, dressed in all white, I cried. There he stood with Carl Lewis, Mark Spitz, Nadia Comenici, Greg Louganis and other champions.

But who was going to light the torch? Minutes later, goose-bumps rising, the champion of all times, Muhammed Ali, trembling from Parkinson's disease, lit the torch. The moment was electric. I will never forget it.

I prayed each time I sat down to write for guidance and truth. It was an emotionally exhausting experience but a spiritually exhilarating one. I knew this was an important book and I had an enormous responsibility. This book through the telling of one life could inspire others. Or why write it?

Bob did not know or recall many things about his family. The deeper the pain, the deeper he buried it. What he did recall or discovered, he expressed strong opinions about. I ordered birth and death certificates and prison records. I questioned him; scolded him; got angry with him and cried for him and his mother. But I did not judge. We pieced together his childhood which was a patchwork quilt of episodes and moments. Some of the names have been changed to respect their privacy. My legal and psychological training helped to organize, uncover, research, recognize behavioral patterns and ask the right questions.

It was therapeutic for both of us. Bob became closer to his maternal family. I appreciated my mother and father even more than I already did. Bob discovered how he fit into the equation and discovered that there was an orchestrated effort to keep him apart from his mother's relatives. Not only did his first cousin, Diane Brown Brisbane, locate an important photograph but he re-discovered his great-aunt, Emmie King, who lives in Harlem.

Throughout the two years it took to research and write this book, spirit made it possible for me to personally meet people and be places that I needed to see. I met a majority of the 1968 Olympic track team including Ralph Boston, Al Oerter, Bill Toomey, Wyomia Tyus, Dick Fosbury, Tommie Smith, Ron Freeman, Lee Evans and others; the late Coach Larry Ellis, Coach Wayne Vandenberg, Igor Ter-Ovanesyan, Dr. Leroy Walker, Tony Duffy, Dick Schaap, Donna DeVarona, the late Coach Stan Wright, Julius Erving, Spanish journalist Miguel Vidal, Bob's maternal uncle, the late Wilbert Brown and his children, percussionist Milford Graves and step-siblings, Nanette Beamon and Chris Beamon and others.

I visited: Estadio Olimpico in Mexico City and discovered it was shaped like a sombrero; Madrid, Spain; UTEP in El Paso, Texas; the Samuel Huntington Housing Projects in South

Jamaica, Queens; Athens, Greece; the house on Mathias Avenue in Queens; McClester Funeral Home; PS40; the 600 school site in Manhattan and more.

I watched hours of video and spent days in research in the libraries and on the Internet.

I want to thank my friend and agent, Janell Walden Agyeman of Marie Brown and Associates, for her tenacity and belief in this project. Many thanks to Gary M. Frazier, Editor-in-Chief of Genesis Press, for his enthusiasm and commitment to this book. Special thanks to Christine Santoro, my executive assistant for all her technical and spiritual support; Charles Burnett for his encouraging words to pursue a book project; Nancy Ancrum for her feedback on the proposal; my friend, author Tananarive Due for sharing; Norma Spector for her painstaking editorial contribution on the original manuscript; Christine Rosa of *Sports Illustrated* for support and research assistance; Louise Argianas, ABC News for archival footage; Michael Maynard in London for archival footage; Dr. Dorothy Holmes, a psychologist in early childhood development and specialist in behavior of at-risk youth; Zoe Lattimer, MSW for professional information about the behavior of abandoned youth; Ralph Boston for insight; Sudie Davis for insight; Joey Walker for insight and research assistance; my sister, Christina Walter Waller for her feedback, love and support; my brother, Willis W. Walter, Jr., Ph.D.-candidate, for his expertise in early childhood development; my mother, Delorese Walter who contributed in more ways than she knows.

This book was a labor of love with the man that I love. A loving thank you to my darling Bob, my hero, for the opportunity to co-author his story and to share with the world that in the game of life, three strikes and you're old does not apply. We just need to keep going until we get it right. God bless.

Milana Walter Beamon
Miami, Florida

Mexico City

October 18, 1968

"Oh say can you see," I started to sing as I thought about the irony of hearing the national anthem played in a stadium shaped like a sombrero. So there I was, "by the dawn's early light what so proudly we hailed at the twilight's last gleaming." There I was representing the United States of America. There I was at the Olympics, standing on the victory stand with a gold medal hanging around my neck and an olive branch wreath in my hand. But I hadn't always been so fortunate. You see, I'd come a long, long way, baby!

Chapter One

Love Child

I couldn't see my hands in front of my face. I trembled with nerves as globs of sweat left transparent streaks running down my cheeks, past my chin and landing on the neck of my hand-me-down blue T-shirt. I was scared.

For once in my life, I acknowledged my vulnerability. That cocky-ass attitude of invincibility abandoned me just like my mother had. Inside I felt alone and empty. Feelings so invisible, so hard to reveal, but, oh so real. The cold steel handcuffs cinched my skinny wrists. Another reality check that I lived in hell, I thought, as I sat quietly in the backseat of the blue-and-white cruiser, sirens blaring. My Virgo haughtiness evaporated when we entered the parking lot of the 103rd Precinct of the New York Police Department.

They fast-walked me into the military-installation prewar building. My feet were only too familiar with those high-gloss, linoleum-floored hallways. In this chaotic, neurotic and psychotic atmosphere, I was low-key compared to the screaming, fighting and sometimes weeping people from all walks of life whom I passed on my way to wherever. They sat me down at a desk and then this cocky, Queens-accented voice came from behind my back: "My name is Detective James White, Homicide Division. You are here because you fit the description of a killer that eyewitnesses saw fleeing from the scene of a murder," he announced with a filterless cigarette hanging from his lips and smoke billowing in his face. My ears no longer heard. I hung on that last word...*Murder. Mur...der? MURDER!!!*

"Hell, I didn't kill nobody!" I declared.

"Can you prove it? So, then, where were you at 1:23 P.M. today? Huh? You sure as hell wasn't in school, Bobby Beamon."

How did he know my name?

"You know, you punks are all the same, always playing dumb and always playing like you're victims of society. Oh, yeah, and you're *always* innocent!" he said as he slapped me upside my head.

I barely felt it. I could hardly breathe—I could hardly see through my eyes. I felt trapped by something in my soul. I would discover much later that I was trapped by what wasn't in my soul.

"Do you eat, boy?" Detective White's question brought me out of the daze.

"Sometimes," I countered.

"A sack of pork rib bones got more meat on them than you have on you. The word's out that you can play that ball. No wonder you can jump so high, you ain't got no weight on you."

My head was about to explode from listening to all this needless chatter, while other police officers and detectives kept bringing him papers and whispering in his ear. There I sat, vulnerable to these idiots in the back room ready to send me up to fry. But this damn detective kept talking and talking and talking, "You know what you need to do, Beamon? You need to jump on the basketball court instead of jumping school." And on and on.

By now the gastric juices in my stomach felt like a geyser had erupted inside of me. I squirmed from side to side in the chair.

Then his phone rang. *Answer the phone! Answer the phone!* I was shouting in my head.

Finally, he picked up the receiver. After a few moments of "ah huhs" and "uh uhs" he hung up.

"You are really lucky, Beamon. You know that? You must have one helluva guardian angel. They caught the killer. You're free to go now." He sounded a bit disappointed. I damn near ran into myself as I scrambled to reach the exit. But his voice followed me. "You'll be back!"

I stared back at him and as I turned my face away from him, the humility disappeared and the growl in my heart reentered just as strong, just as mean and just as deadly as it was before. I was fourteen years old with a hole in my soul.

* * *

I wondered how her voice would have sounded, how I would have felt when she held me, how her lips would have felt when she kissed me, what her scent would have been like. One dream was particularly vivid and I remember certain details of it to this very day.

The features of her face were vague, flooded by the radiance of the white light that surrounded her image in my mind. She spoke in a whisper and I strained to hear the words coming from her mouth.

"I didn't want to leave you, baby, but it was time for me to go. You might not understand now, but always remember you are someone very, very special. And baby, you will always be in my soul and in my heart. Always."

* * *

Her voice faded, and I awakened. I wondered, *Who was my mother, Naomi Brown Beamon?* It was a question that remained mostly unanswered until I was damn-near 35. There was always so little ever said about my mother that she lingered in my mind as a dreamlike figure: mysterious and mystical. So, later in life, I found myself attempting to make ghosts talk and force old minds to recall details that had been washed away by time. My mother had an unusual relationship with my grandmother, Bessie, who was her mother-in-law. When I was hunting around for old hospital records on my mother, my grandmother became very uneasy with my quest for information.

I had just returned to New York after living in Madrid for a year. I had promised myself, that as soon as I came back to the States I was going to find out more about my mother. When I called and told Ma (her name was Bessie) what I wanted to know, there was a long silence on the phone. She told me I needed to come see her. I was nervous and confused. Would she tell me something more than I already knew about my mother?

* * *

Ma lived in Queens but was house-sitting for a friend who lived on Strivers Row; only blacks who had money used to live on Strivers Row. Ma was in her seventies then, with mocha-colored skin, pleasingly plump, five foot two, dressed in a reddish-purple silk shirtwaist dress that complimented her black, shoulder-length wig. She liked to consider herself fashionable. She was an Eastern Star, the sister organization of the Masons, and I believe she had reached the highest degree. But she also read tea leaves and coffee grounds, played numbers every day, gambled at the racetrack and made a ritual of reading the Sunday edition of *The Daily News* each week from cover to cover. Her friend was visiting family in Connecticut for a few days. Ma had friends and family in Harlem, so being there was almost like being on vacation. The walls of the clean but overly furnished brownstone apartment were wallpapered with family photographs and portraits; some recent ones but also many vintage ones from the 1800s, the 1920s and 1940s...maybe there was one of my mother. But that was ridiculous, why would there be a picture of my mother here?

"Shucks. Oh my, Bobby. Boy, look at them clothes. Ya got to be really somethin'. Lookin' so nice, like one of them yella haughty Negroes! Ya come and sit down now. Want a cup of coffee? I just made it, fresh. Ya mama loved coffee; she used to drink it all the time."

"I love coffee, too, Ma, *I* drink it all the time."

Her whole demeanor felt peculiar. She was fidgety and rarely made eye contact. She had never been an affectionate person anyway, but this was different. It was strange, very strange; a feeling I can't put into words.

"Ma, I never remember you calling me yellow before." We both got a good laugh out of that. We needed a little humor to break the tension.

When she came back from the kitchen with the coffee, she told me that my mother confided in her and shared intimate details that she had never shared with anyone else. I wondered why she had never told me about my mother before.

But I contained myself because I didn't want to distract her from giving me this information. I had waited long enough. My heart pounded with anticipation as I sat back in an old upholstered wingback chair and crossed my legs. She sat across from me, sunk down in a brocaded love seat. Then she leaned toward me, looking over her half-moon eyeglasses; I felt like I was being tucked in for a bedtime story and that she was Mother Goose—except I knew better. So I braced myself for a Stephen King nightmare instead. From that moment on I was completely under her spell.

"Now I want ya to listen real good, Bobby, 'cause I ain't gonna tell this twice. I didn't think that I would ever have to tell this. I hadn't thought about Naomi in so many years. But I truly believe that things happen for a reason...and there must be some real good reason why ya have come to me with these questions after all these years. So, I'm gonna tell ya everything that I know and everything that Naomi told me herself.

"Yo mama was a baby her own self. Her mama died soon after she had her. Naomi felt unwanted at home. But she knew nuthin' about the real world. Nuthin'. All she knew was that she wanted to get away from her daddy and stepmama. Naomi told me that her stepmama couldn't stand her and was always beatin' up on her. Lookin' at ya, Bobby, is bringin' to mind lots of thangs like it was yesterday. I remember the first time I saw ya. Shoot, it was so hot and sticky that day in August of 1946. Ya had just been born and was kickin' and carryin' on in that crib in the middle of the nursery ward at Queens Hospital. Ya little tiny arms was always reachin' in the air seemed like for yo mama who wasn't there. I passed by just as ya seemed to reach to me through the glass. All I could do was wave to ya," she said. "Yeah, Bobby, I was right there from the start."

I could hardly swallow. What the hell was happening here? I couldn't believe what I was hearing. She had never told me about this before. The fact was, I had never seen any baby pictures of myself. Questions to myself were shooting rapidly through my ears. "Please go on," I told her.

Ma paused for a minute with a blank stare on her face. Then she took a sip of her coffee and continued to talk, her eyes looking at me but looking past me, if you know what I mean.

"Down the hall in a quarantine ward, away from all the other mamas, yo mama was a sickly little thang who was as short as me and in her twenties. That girl had this smooth, cocoa-brown skin and thick, straight, black, good hair, all the way down her shoulders. Oh, but when I saw her that day, them almond-shaped eyes was stretched open in terror and wet with tears as she twisted and turned in her bed. She begged with her eyes to the eyes of the nurses, who wore them masks. She was so scared and so alone; the orderlies had to wrestle her down and hold her to keep her from gettin' out the bed. It was awful to see her tug and moan. Her body was soaked with perspir'-tion, as she fought to breathe and cough up tablespoons of blood at the same time. But even with all this goin' on, even though she had no more energy, that mother's instinct gave her strength enough to scream, 'Where's my baby? Where's my baby? I want to hold my baby! Nurse, please, please tell me, where is my baby?'"

I said, "Ma, how come you've decided to tell me about my mother now? All these years I have wondered. All these years you have led me to believe that you didn't know much about her and all along you knew the answers! Ma, how could you have kept this from me, and why had you wanted to?"

I lost it! I couldn't stop shaking my head as tears streamed from my eyes and blurred my vision.

Ma looked like a shadow sitting across from me. I could feel her patting me on the knee in an attempt to calm me down. She did not address my outburst and just continued on with her story as if nothing had happened, just like she did when I was a kid, every time I asked about my mother.

"Hush, hush, now."

Ma shook her head and told me that she had blocked this sadness completely from her mind long ago, but that her heart remembered. She let her emotions flow and wiped her tears as I tried to hold mine back.

"Lord, Lord, Lord! In a few weeks, ya was much bigger than all the other babies in the ward. Ya looked so sad, Bobby. Babies was comin' and goin'. The doctors and the nurses was exhausted from all the overtime work. Ya know, it was right after the war and no one had never experienced nuthin' like this before. Ya see it was baby-boom time and babies was all over the place. But for ya and yo mama, none of that stuff mattered. I believe ya could sense that yo mama had not been there to see ya or hold ya. By now, it was the middle of September. Ya ain't felt your mama's warm body and the sound of her heart beatin' next to yo's, ya ain't seen her eyes, touched her hair or rubbed yo tiny hands across her face. Even as a baby, I believe that there was a connection that cried for attention that never came. It seemed to me the nurses was nice and looked out for ya as much as they could, but they had so many babies to take care of and the new babies kept cumin' and cumin' and cumin'. Whenever I could git to the hospital, ya seemt to always reach for dear life toward any voice ya could hear, somehow expectin' that somebody would pick ya up and take ya out of there. Bobby, it seemt to me like everyone on the floor was worried about ya. Them nurses tried to protect ya from being taken by the State by movin' ya around and hidin' ya so that their bosses wouldn't get suspicious, since ya had been there so long."

At this point, I did not have words to say, was this my story? My grandmother frowned to herself for a second, but when she looked at me again, I blinked and nodded for her to continue. She sighed.

"Every now and then, I would come up there to check on ya. The nurses knew me and let me come to see you even if it was way past visitin' hours. This black nurse, I can't remember her name, had an earful for me when she saw me one Sunday. 'Just how long do you intend to keep this baby here? Don't you realize that this child needs to be held and kissed and to be with his mother, or you, or someone who's going to love him?' she said to me. I nodded and promised her that I would be back to take ya in a few days. She then promised me that if I didn't come back, she had already called the State Department of Child Welfare and told them that there may be an abandoned baby up there and she would have them take you, if necessary! That woman didn't like me. She didn't know what was goin' on.

"Naomi said for me to swear to God that I would take care of her baby when she died. She made me swear on the Bible. This promise, of course, made things very messy for me. Naomi was out of the hospital then and at home with me, but still fightin' with the tuberculosis...while ya were still in the nursery. Naomi would tell me later that right after ya was born, her life was a blur—unreal but real.

"'I'm so ashamed, Jesus,' she told me. 'My baby just don't deserve this kind of life. Now, you've gotta help me, Bessie. Something is suckin' the air outta me... Oh, Jesus, I can't leave here in peace 'less I know you—swear—to—take—care—of—Rob—ert...' Naomi would try to talk but her words would come in between her coughin' and tremblin'. Then I would rub her shakin' hands, and watch her, disbelievin' that this was happenin' to someone so young, right before my very eyes."

The way she was telling me this, I felt like I was actually there, that I had traveled back in time thirty-five years. I could feel my mother's anguish and see the confusion in my grandmother's eyes. It was a strange sensation, but my heart thirsted for more. Ma was really into it, too; the scenes were flowing from her mouth as if all this had happened yesterday.

"Yo mama was born and raised in Long Island. She told me all about herself after she married my boy, James. Her daddy was a hardworkin' man, who kept a neat and clean roof over her and her brother, Wilbert's head. When Naomi was an arm baby, this was before her real mama died, she fell out of her high chair and broke her face. Them doctors took out the broken bones and just sewed up her face. So she had this ugly scar on her face and she ain't had no cheekbone there.

"Her daddy remarried and her stepmama was mean and beat her and Wilbert. Naomi was quiet and kept to herself but she had created her own little dream world inside her head. She had the notion that just 'cause she could jitterbug, she could be famous like the girls who danced in Harlem and in the Broadway chorus lines. She never knew that she had to go to dancin' school or that she had to go to tryouts. Seemt like Naomi did not know what to do with herself, so, she got herself caught up with my son, James, whose claim to fame was hustlin' and pimpin'. He thought he was half-ass good-lookin' then. Naomi married him against her brother, Wilbert's wishes. James was nothing but a triflin', nappy-headed, no-good scoundrel then! In her dream world inside her head, yo mama ain't had no sense.

"Still with me, Bobby?" Ma asked, probably sensing that I had floated off somewhere else and wanting to make sure I was paying attention.

"I'm still here" I answered, and she continued.

"Ya know that fo' years before ya was born, Naomi and James's son, yo half-brother, Andrew, was born. When the nurse brought the baby to her after a hellified delivery, she was stunned but not entirely surprised—Andrew's head was deformed, and he was epileptic. That day, yo mama's doctor told her to her face that her body was just too weak to have anymo' children, her body was too weak for the strain of child-birth. But there was more to it than that, and she and I knew somethin' that the doctor didn't."

What a great storyteller Ma was. I found myself hanging on her every word. But did she really have to keep all these stories from me for all these years?

"Now, Bobby, if this is too much, I don't have to go on."

I told her it was okay. Now that she was so into it, I did not want her to stop. All this secretive and superstitious mumbo jumbo about not talking about dead people because they could come back to haunt you had run its course with me. I needed her to go on. There had already been too many years of not knowing about my family. At this point, I didn't care why things had happened, I just wanted to know who, what and where.

She smoothed her dress and shifted around a little on the love seat. She appeared a bit nervous.

"Even I am surprised how long this stuff has kept in my head. Like it was just waitin' fo' me to press the right button fo' it to come out. God sure works in mysterious ways, huh? Ya know James was my only one. What ya don't know is that James hardly saw his daddy 'cause his daddy lived with his other family in Brooklyn. He and I lived in Queens. But, by the time he was twelve, he was drinkin', gamblin', stealin' and pimpin' older women. That man would not work to save a lick. Always robbin' Peter to pay Paul. He was a heavy drinker who got mean and evil after he had that whiskey, just like what happened to Dr. Jekyll after he drank that potion and he turned into Mr. Hyde. James was always drunk when he used yo mama as his punchin' bag.

"One time about four in the mornin', James had been out all night, partyin' and drinkin' and gamblin'. Yo mama had been up all night hungry and waitin' for him to come home with some groceries. She was seven months pregnant with Andrew. It had been meatless Friday, Tuesday was the other meatless day, when the war was goin' on. Shoot, we ain't had no meat in the first place, to have meatless days! No way we could've even had a pound and a half of meat each week. Yeah, that was the limit during the war. Anyway, Friday was also payday for James. Since he was an ex-convict, he couldn't serve in the military, so he got a job workin' in the war plant in Astoria that made the uniforms for the soldiers. Ev'rybody knew that them jobs paid real good money, but Naomi never saw none of it.

"But by now she must have been beside herself from havin' no sleep and no food. I'm sure them hormones had shot up to the heavens, too. Then James stumbled in, damp and stankin' of whiskey, cigarette smoke and perfume. I woke up when I heard yo mama yellin' about where he had been and complainin' that there was no food in the house, because he still hadn't brought none home.

"I got up and saw him circlin' her chair in the kitchen and yellin', 'Who the hell do ya think ya's talkin' to, bitch? I'll kick yo narrow ass!'

"'You best not have spent all the money on whiskey and your whores.' Naomi told him. But before she could finish the sentence, James had jumped over to the chair where she was sittin', and with his closed fist socked her with an uppercut punch so hard that it knocked her off the chair and onto the floor, just like Joe Louis used to fight.

"As she tried desperately to crawl away from him on all fours, he ran over to her and kicked her over and over again in her pregnant belly. I grabbed James from the back, tryin' to keep him from hurtin' her more. Then he turned on me and started slappin' me with his open hands. Naomi took an empty Seagram's V.O. whiskey bottle, broke it with one hand, held her stomach with the other hand and was just 'bout to stab James in his back with the broken bottle when I saw her, standin' frozen behind him with her eyes stretched open in a daze like someone gone crazy. It was scary. I begged her, 'Naomi, don't kill my son. Please don't kill him.' She couldn't hear me. Her body was in that room but her mind was gone somewhere else. She screamed, 'I'm gonna kill you, you bastard! I'm tired of you treatin' me like I'm your slave, a dog in the street that you kick and spit on. I'm tired!' I caught her arm in midair...just missed stabbin' James by inches. Bobby, I had to pry her bloody fingers off of the neck of the whiskey bottle, one by one. Her grip had been the grip of death. She saw that time in her mind when she held little Andrew, she told me. Somethin' happened to Naomi that day at the hospital: somethin' deep and secret. It was really very, very strange."

I got up and walked over to the window that looked out onto the row of brownstones on 137th Street. I just needed to move around. This was not the first time that I had felt betrayed by Ma. Here she was playing God with my life; choosing what to tell me, when to tell me, and how to tell me. My mother had gone through hell and I should have been told that a long time ago so that I could have understood. Now I finally knew that when she left me, it wasn't because of anything I had done to her.

Ma walked over to a bookshelf and picked up this old book with the face of a Hindu Indian on the cover. It was her dream book. I hadn't seen that damn thing in years. Then she told me that she had had a dream last night that she didn't understand until she found the interpretation in her book.

"It was well into autumn 1946. Come to think of it, it was October, and ya had been born the last week of August. Shucks, ya looked like a toddler compared to them other babies in the nursery. Ya had them long legs with muscles in them, and ya stood out from all the rest. I couldn't stop thinkin' about ya all alone in that place. And on that day, I picked ya up from the crib. Ya grabbed my shoulders as tight as ya could. I was walkin' fast through the hospital hallway and had just passed a stone-faced woman who was walkin' toward the nursery. I ran down them steps, out the door, into the fresh air. I flagged down a cab, and we went uptown. I tell you, Bobby, it was meant to be. I found out later that that woman was the social worker comin' to get you to take you away. I didn't know the social worker was comin' that day. But I must have felt somethin', 'cause I got ya outta there just in the nick of time!

I couldn't help thinking what a disaster all this was! My mother left me in the hospital. She was sick. I was not her husband's baby. She had me by a lover. She didn't know what to do. James was serving his third year in Sing-Sing when I was conceived. When he was paroled, my mother was almost eight months pregnant with me. So when I was born, no one in James's family wanted to claim me. But Ma had eventually promised my mother that she would take care of me. What a complicated mess!

"Ya know, Bobby, ya ain't got no control on how ya come into this world. Ya take the hand that life has dealt ya and play it as best ya can. See, what had happened, James had made it known to yo mama when he came back home from prison that he didn't want nothin' to do with ya. She and I had secretly worked out that I would take ya to stay with Aunt Carly. Carly used the insurance money that Harry left her to make her three-story brownstone on Convent Avenue into a roomin' house. Her husband, Harry, died just like that one day from a heart attack while trying to take down Christmas lights from the roof. Po' thing. Harry was a good man, bless his soul.

"Anyway, her boarders included 'outside children;' children born outside of marriage. That's what they called them, among other...anyway, Harlem was miles away from Queens for Naomi. She would call Carly when she could to find out how you was doin' and ask if Carly would kiss and hold ya for her. But, Bobby, Carly was a businesswoman, not a babysitter, and she kept ya clean and fed, and that was 'bout the best that she could do. I would come and see ya when I'd come over to pay her ev'ry month. Yo mama had been too weak to travel and she couldn't tell anyone that she wanted to go to Harlem 'cause she was scared that James would find out where ya was and maybe do somethin' crazy to ya and to her. He was still drinkin' that whiskey like a fish, you know. It was terrible."

Ma started rocking back and forth like some people do in church when the Spirit moves them. She was pressing that dream book close to her body. She closed her eyes as she continued to speak. I started to feel even more uncomfortable.

"I remember that day in the middle of May so clearly, the day she finally was able to get to go to Harlem. The sun shined so bright. It was a good day for Naomi. She felt much stronger than she had in a long time, and she hardly coughed. Her girlfriend Ruthie had promised to drive us to Harlem to see ya. 'You got the camera, for sure, Ruthie?' she kept askin' over and over. Ruthie and I was tickled pink from Naomi's excitement. I showed her the camera so that yo mama could shut her mouth about it. When we got to Carly's, Naomi's eyes got big as saucers when she seen yo with them long legs. I think ya was about nine months old then. I don't know much about what was on her mind, but she was so happy to see ya that she lifted ya, with her skinny little arms, hugged ya and spun around with ya. She held ya still long enough to pose for the picture that Ruthie took with her camera. Ruthie and I was so happy for her but so sad that her happiness would only be for a few minutes 'cause Naomi had danced herself sick and had to be careful not to cough on ya or anybody else."

"Wait a minute, wait a minute, Ma! You were with my mother when she took that photograph? Don't you remember? You told me my mother had never held me because she was so sick. All these years, I thought we had never touched each other? Why didn't you tell me about this before? Where is the photograph? This is so much to digest, Ma, all these years...I have wondered."

"Oh, that picture's long gone. Besides, all that stuff was nothin' for ya to worry 'bout. Bobby, ya is old enough to understand this now, but life is just too short. Life can get real hard, and I made what happened into teachers who showed me how to live and others who taught me how not to live. I changed my life. I had so much goin' on. Two months after she took that picture with ya, Naomi was taken to Triboro Hospital and sent to ward 7A. It was the same hospital that she had worked in while James was in prison.

"The nurses and the doctors frowned as sweat dropped from their foreheads. 'Hang on, Naomi, don't give up now. Just hang on,' the nurses told me they whispered in her ear. But, they could just feel that yo mama had her own plans. She told me a few days before she died that her life played in her mind like when she watched one of those picture shows: seein' herself as a little girl growin' up in Long Island, switchin' her narrow little hips and poppin' her fingers to Bessie Smith songs playin' on the radio and gettin' her behind beat by her stepma-ma for listenin' to 'devil's music.' She saw her weddin' day when James disappeared for hours, and her brother told her that James had gone to be with some old girlfriend; she thought about the time when he had kicked Andrew while he was still in her stomach and that scary time that her mind snapped.

"Then she said that her mind got real quiet and she told me her most special memories: She said she saw it so clear, the first time she saw yo real daddy, who also worked at Triboro Hospital. Yo mama was a real good old soul. I don't like to talk too much about the dead. Naomi had told me for months about this tall black man who, she said, was a doctor, and how she admired him. He was from some place I don't remember, and she would say how handsome he was and how his skin looked like mahogany velvet. She was just a nurse's aide, ya know, and was a little ashamed that she didn't finish school. Ain't none of that mattered to him, she told me, he was always respectful and polite—and always busy. She asked me not to think bad of her for wanting to be with someone else, but I was glad to see her smile for a change after what James had put her through. But after all, if truth be told, she was a married woman. The doctor did not know that, though.

"Yeah, Naomi told me that they had a thang for each other. I was the only one she'd talk to. She was very shy and had sadness in her eyes, even when she smiled. But when she would see him, oh my goodness, she'd come home with eyes so bright they could light up the world. One day, he found out that it was her birthday and she told me about this rose that he gave her. Then, the Christmas holidays had started and the workers was tradin' shifts in order to finish their shoppin' and to spend time with their families. Naomi volunteered to work the graveyard shifts on Christmas Eve, Christmas Day and New Year's Eve, switchin' her usual late-night shift with co-workers. She told me that it was better to work than be home cryin' the blues over havin' a convict for a husband and a retarded son who she could not help.

"It was Christmas that they got together. She wasn't sorry that they got together at all, she told me. He wished her a Merry Christmas and gave her a small gift box tied with a wide red bow. She remembered that so well 'cause James hardly ever gave her presents. She couldn't believe it. He carried her to a linen closet. She knew it was a special night. She had sex standing up with him and she told me that she knew they had made ya that night. For yo mama, it was something she would never, ever forget. He had bought her a beautiful marcasite locket. He hung it around her neck and kissed her hair. Two days later, she heard he had been transferred to a hospital in Los Angeles. She said they never saw each other again. She never tried to reach him when her stomach got big with ya inside. I never knew his name and I never asked."

I was stunned by the revelation about my biological father—absolutely stunned. This was the first time that I had ever heard anything about the man who fathered me. Suddenly, I was thirsty.

"Ma, I need something," I finally said, feeling overwhelmed by all that I had heard. She dropped this on me so casually. I felt all these different emotions cramping in my stomach: rage, disappointment, sadness, grief, disgust. But you know people in those days were always keeping secrets. You know, the what-you-don't-know-won't-hurt-you generation. I had to settle down. I had to get out of there real quick.

"Bobby, your mama danced herself sick," Ma went on. "She danced at nightclubs all the time. She would be hot and sweaty and then go outside without a coat—in the dead of winter. Her life was nuthin' like she thought it would be, but seemt like she had dreams for ya. As the doctors tried to keep her alive, I believe that all Naomi could think of was 'lettin' go'. The nurses said they could see it on her face and in her eyes. She was ready to go home to the Lord. She had no more business left. She must have known in her heart that she had nuthin' to lose by havin' her love child; at least ya daddy was somebody special. I believe her mother's instinct knew that ya was goin' to be someone very, very special. She told me she would tell ya that over and over as you grew in her stomach and she would rub ya as ya would move inside her.

"The nurse on duty told me that Naomi took her last breath in the early mornin'. When she passed away, a veil of peace smoothed out the pain on her face. People who see death all the time know that look. The sign of life that the doctors fought so hard to see in Naomi's body, came another way: death. Naomi gave the Lord permission to take her soul. The peace on her face was her sign. She had ya even though her doctors told her that doing so could kill her, even though she was married and expectin' a baby by another man, even though her heart was broken, even though the tuberculosis was slowly killin' her. Now, she could rest, she could go home to the Lord. Ya know, Bobby, I will never forget yo mama. She was so little but so strong."

She took a deep breath as she leaned back on the love seat. There was dead silence in the room. I got up to put on my coat. I told my grandmother I had an appointment in midtown in twenty minutes. All I wanted to do was get out of there. I kissed her on the forehead, hugged her even though she hardly hugged back, and thanked her for finally telling me. When I got outside, I was so enraged that it wasn't until I reached Zabar's that I realized I had walked more than fifty blocks.

My mother died from tuberculosis when she was twenty-five years old and I was eleven months.

That same year, the Mayo Clinic discovered the streptomycin that could have saved her.

Chapter Two

Dreams Come True?

My mother was so young when she died. I wondered what her funeral was like. Was I there? Did anyone think to come to Aunt Carly's to get me? At that very moment when my mother's spirit left her body, did my body feel like her body felt? Just limp and left behind? Was I scared? Did I shudder? Those are questions whose answers are lost in time, but perhaps present in my heart—if not, why would I bother to wonder? Even though I was only eleven months old, I am positive that the passing of my mother induced sensations of angst in my little soul.

Remembering when Ma told me that Naomi danced herself sick, it seemed to me that my mother must've danced herself to death. Like she was following a death wish.

"James killed her just as if he had put a gun to her head and pulled the trigger," Uncle Wilbert said, when he told me about the funeral. He told me that she was laid out in a purple satin dress. That she looked like a little girl asleep waiting to be awakened by a kiss. She was so young, lying there, baby-faced and free. She had been in Triboro Hospital for twenty-three days. Finally at 7:30 A.M. on July 31, 1947, she let go.

My mother left me and I believe I felt her disappear. My mother's brother, Uncle Wilbert, was at her funeral. It took him damn-near fifty years to tell me about it—and he only spoke of it because I asked him about it, point-blank. It had taken me so long to have the presence of mind to ask any questions about her and about what happened back then. Perhaps I avoided the questions in anticipation of being disappointed or maybe I just feared that I didn't know how I would react and might be out of control. But who the hell knows?

Uncle Wilbert was in his seventies now, still living in Queens. His wife, Carrie, died when I was a kid. I remember her well, though. I thought she was the prettiest woman I had ever seen. She was petite, light-brown skinned with dark hair and real pretty eyes and a warm smile. They had five children, Audrey, Diane, Russell, Wilbert, Jr., and Buzzy. Diane was my favorite. She seemed to talk to me more. Take more time with me. Plus, she was the spitting image of her mother. They were my first cousins on my mother's side but it never felt that close, even though they lived down the street from me.

"At your mother's funeral, people were whispering and gossiping about James's messin' around," Uncle Wilbert told me, still talking about the funeral.

His tone grew angrier. Made me think that James and my mother were the talk of the neighborhood. I could picture the kind of folks that were there—drinking and laughing and eating and loud-talking like it was their last meal or something. I've been around people like that before. To them, every gathering with food and whiskey was a party.

While we were talking, my cousin Diane had taken out all these family photos, interrupting Uncle Wilbert's conversation with her questions. "Don't you remember her?" or "Do you remember when we were here?" Then she pulled a black and white photograph out of the stack.

"Bobby, here's a picture of you and your mother."

My reaction was far from remarkable, as I held it in my hand. I was completely numb. It wasn't "long gone" as Ma had believed. I guess I'm saying all this to say that when I studied that photograph of my mother and absorbed every detail—her fingers, her shoulders, her nose (I don't have her nose, I thought), her hair (I used to have her hair), her smooth skin, her dress, her shoes...but when I looked at her eyes, they seemed sad and glad, all at once.

I must have been heavy for her to hold. My legs were long and dangling even then, at about nine months old. The expression on my face looked as if someone had interrupted where I wanted my eyes to be with a "Bobby, look at the camera. Now smile and say cheese." I looked annoyed and confused in that photograph. My mother was pressing me close to her with both her arms wrapped tightly around me. Anyway, I kept thinking about that photograph, and the picture in my mind of her stretched out in a coffin at twenty-five years young.

It took until 1997 for Uncle Wilbert to be able to talk to me about it. He said that her service was sad for many reasons. Some people were sobbing and just staring at Naomi in disbelief that she was really dead. The place was hot. It was August 4th in New York City. I could picture church-dressing New York black folks, stylish and respectful, trying to survive the sweltering heat and humidity by fanning themselves into a sweat with those thin cardboard church fans attached to a Popsicle-wood handle.

"James was a dirty bastard. There he was at his wife's funeral and I'm looking at my baby sister laying in that damn box and I wanted to kill him," Uncle Wilbert told me in a voice just above a whisper.

He said that there was so much peace on her face but so much static in the chapel. James was outside McClester Funeral Home on New York Boulevard, with whiskey smelling all on his breath. He pulled Uncle over to the side to tell him about how "good a lay" this other woman was. That was his conversation to his brother-in-law who knew how James had beat her and mistreated her and then ended up leaving her for four years with a brain-damaged baby, no money, no nothing—while he was up there in the penitentiary.

He was strutting around like the head rooster of the henhouse. I tried to imagine such a thing: James trying to drown his guilt with whiskey and Uncle holding back his rage with painful restraint. What a dubious tribute to my mother.

But where was I? I stayed at Aunt Carly's rooming house until 1951 when I was five years old. I had two friends there, Dee Dee and Buddy. Someone would always come and pick them up on the weekends and I would be the only kid left behind then. I remember I would sit in the window and watch the grown-ups on Convent Avenue walking to work, or sweeping their stoops or talking with other neighbors. I remember these two older ladies, I guess they were sisters, who would have their radio blaring music all day; this was way before the days of the ghetto-blasters. I'd sing along with the radio, "Rag Mop. R-A-G-M-O-P. Rag Mop!" Maybe those were the first words I'd learned to spell. But I also liked to listen to the episodes of "Amos & Andy," "The Shadow" and "The Whistler" on the radio. For some reason, I remember that so clearly.

I was a little more than a number at Aunt Carly's. I would see Ma every now and then. Oh, Aunt Carly kept me clean and I never recall being without food. But my heart was hungry for love, affection and attention. I would see Dee and Buddy get picked up and hugged when their family would come get them on weekends. I just wanted somebody to do that to me. I guess lots of children feel invisible—no one listens, no one sees, no one touches.

"When is Ma comin', Aunt Carly? Is it today? Isn't today the day?" I would ask over and over. By then, I was about five and Aunt Carly would warn me about getting on her nerves with all those questions. Then she would dismiss me by telling me to go somewhere and play.

One day I was moping around and walked past Mr. Moore's room. Mr. Moore looked to be about fifty-something—fifty was old to me. He had been living at Aunt Carly's for as long as I could remember. He practiced his blackjack techniques on me, pushing and hitting me with it, taunting me as he slapped the thing on the palm of his hand.

"This is how they treat *bad* people," he said.

This particular time when I walked by, Mr. Moore was singing to himself in the mirror; slicking back his *lye-fried hair* that was plastered to his skull with Royal Crown Pomade. I was watching his every move through the cracked door, curious about the aftershave lotion that he splashed on his razor-bumped face and neck. He must have felt me watching. He casually reached into his top dresser drawer, pulled out the blackjack, turned and caught me right in my eyes. Man, I was stunned. I could not move I was so surprised.

"You see this?" he asked as he slapped that damn blackjack on his palm.

My eyes bugged out of my head and I hauled ass, just like a frightened Rochester in a Jack Benny movie.

"Now stay from aroun' here, you nasty lil' bastard," he said.

I could not stop thinking about that. Days had gone by and I was still thinking about Mr. Moore and his damn blackjack. So one night, I snuck into Mr. Moore's room while he was asleep. In between his deafening snores, I tiptoed ever so quietly to his dresser. I reached up, opened the top drawer, slid out the small leather-covered wood club from under his underwear, did a dry run with a couple of slaps on my hand, walked to the bed and whacked him all over his back and arm, with all the might of an angry, revenge-seeking five-year-old. *I* showed *him* what they do to *bad* people.

That's what I thought. Suddenly, he jumped out of the bed and chased me down the hall. I ran as fast as my five-year-old legs could. But he caught me. He lifted me under my armpits and slammed me up against the wall, all the while shouting, "Black lil' m.f.!" I was kicking and screaming, trying to get away. Then, just as he was about to punch me with his fist, Aunt Carly came between us and begged him not to hurt me.

"I'm goin' to kill this little black m.f.," he said.

"Please don't kill him, Mr. Moore. Please let him go. Just don't kill him. He's only a boy," she pleaded.

The next day, as fate would have it, just as Mr. Moore was probably plotting how to dispose of my little ass, Ma came to take me home with her—for good. I was one happy little kid: I had thousands of butterflies fluttering in my stomach and millions of smiles bubbling up in my heart. Now I was just like Dee Dee and Buddy, I didn't have to worry anymore. Someone wanted to take me home, too.

Mr. Moore was mumbling something as Aunt Carly gathered my belongings and put them in a brown shopping bag. If he were alive today, I wouldn't hesitate to kick his ass.

I was so excited about leaving there that I couldn't think for asking ten questions at once. Where did she live? Was it far? I asked question after question. My only answer was, "Hush, boy."

But that was all right with me. We took the subway and then a bus to Jamaica, Queens. I remember wondering why people were putting money in the boxes. I had never been on a subway or bus before. When we got to Mathias Avenue, we stopped at this big dark-colored house and walked up the steps to the front door. Ma unlocked the door. It was dark inside. There was a man I had never seen before standing in my path. When I looked up at him, he frowned. But I was used to people frowning, so a frown meant nothing to me.

"Gimme somethin' to drink," I blurted out.

To this day, I don't know where that came from. Maybe in my nervousness, I just had to break that awful silence. Maybe. But it also was an indication of the extent of my social graces.

I keep remembering how dark it was. Whether it was actually dark or metaphorically dark, I cannot say. It felt like I was just *put* in there. Not taken there or invited there, but just put there. No one really looked at me or spoke to me. I felt just like a stranger off the street.

Then I saw a boy who was bigger than I was, but not by much. He had spit drooling from his mouth and all down the front of his shirt. He was running around all over the place much like a hamster running on a wheel. He walked with a limp and he made sounds instead of spoken words.

Ma called him Andrew, so I called him Andrew. Ma called her father Pop, so I called him Pop. No one ever told me nothing. Ma, Andrew and I slept in the same bed. Andrew would kick and fight in his sleep most of the night. Ma would leave in the morning and not come home until late at night.

Hillary Taylor was Pop's real name. He was in his eighties when I met him. He was short, dark-skinned, bald-headed and always wore suspenders with his big baggy pants. When he wasn't chewing tobacco and spitting it out in a tin can that he kept by his chair, he was puffing on one of those big fat cigars that stank up the place. He and Ma came to New York from Gates, North Carolina. I don't know why or when.

I remember seeing the Benny "Kid" Peret and Emo Griffith fight on television when Kid Peret got killed in the ring. I remember those, "What'll you have? Pabst Blue Ribbon, Pabst Blue Ribbon Beer" commercials between rounds and the long-legged, dancing Lucky Strikes cigarette boxes. I found familiarity in television, a coziness and kind of closeness. I'd become one with the images before my eyes and all that was around me then became the fantasy. I would laugh. I would sing along with the music. I would watch how other people lived. TV lightened up my darkness. It was my Shangri-la.

The details of how I spent my days are hazy. But I do recall that I had almost the same feeling I had at Aunt Carly's: I still wasn't *included* anywhere. You have to think about what it meant to be a bastard then, in the 1940s and 1950s. Even Shakespeare wrote poems about bastards being lowlifes. And think about what it meant to be a bastard child living with the mother and grandfather of the husband whose wife had a baby by another man and then you've got the story behind the story.

They say that blood is thicker than mud.

I sensed that Pop didn't like me. It was like he was just there to give us lunch and then call it a day. He would walk around the neighborhood pushing a cart and collecting junk. Andrew and I were called "scoundrels" every time we made a noise. I guess we were noisy kids. But Andrew had a close relationship with Pop; I didn't.

Then came school. Kindergarten was a new experience for me in many ways. I was bubbling with excitement to be with other kids. At the very least, I had the attention of grown-ups for a few hours a day. Andrew had been sick a lot and when he would go into his epileptic seizures, Pop struggled to put a spoon in his mouth to keep him from swallowing his tongue. Ma would rub him down with rubbing alcohol. I never understood how he could swallow his tongue. I had tried to do it myself. Sometimes Andrew would scare me when he would jerk and cough up spit. Sometimes he'd just be walking and then he'd fall down to the floor and his whole body would start these violent gyrations. The expression on his face I can still see. He would look so weird with his features distorted and his eyes blank like nothing was behind them. He was nine years old.

Against the noise of the play-by-plays from the baseball games and the cheering crowd on TV or the radio, I would play outside with Andrew's toys and hope inside that he would not get upset. I had no toys of my own and Andrew would snatch his toys from me when I tried to play with him. I just wanted to play; I just wanted to "talk to" the toys.

Thinking back now, I imagine that I was overly playful at school: buzzing around everyone, tickling the girls and hiding toys from the other boys. I heard lots of, "Sit down, Robert Beamon" and "be quiet, Robert Beamon" from my teachers— but they were paying attention to me so that was just fine with me. I was definitely not invisible to them.

I loved it when we would all get together in a circle to sing and clap. My favorite songs were, "The Farmer in the Dell" and "Here We Go Loopdy-Loo." Amazing how the mind works, huh? Amazing that I remember that so clearly. I guess that's why they say that a child's early years are so important in the building of his foundation.

I loved to sing, but my favorite game was Show and Tell. Each and every morning, that's how Mrs. Kinney would start our day, and it was the only time I would sit quietly without anyone having to tell me to sit still. I'd watch intently while the other kids would "show" house keys, coffee cups, newspapers—stuff from their houses. Sometimes the show stuff would be boring, but occasionally someone would get creative, like Joel. I remember when Joel brought Hershey Kisses for everyone for his show and tell. Man, Joel was the most popular kid in class that day; everybody wanted to play with him and share their toys with him. He got so much attention. So, when my turn came I wanted to hit a home run, too. I wanted to be unforgettable.

That morning, I was all smiles. You know how your stomach can bubble when you're a kid and you just can't *wait?* Well, that's how I felt.

"Robert Beamon, are you ready for Show and Tell?" Mrs. Kinney asked.

"Yes, ma'am," I answered as I stood up and dragged my little satchel to the head of the class. I had never felt so confident. I stood still, anxious to bask in my moment of glory. Then, finally, Mrs. Kinney told me to show. I quickly unbuckled the straps and whipped out:

a switchblade
a .38 Smith & Wesson
a handful of bullets

bam, bam, bam—in rapid succession. The other kids gasped and before I could shine in the light of my fifteen minutes of fame—it was all over.

Mrs. Kinney's mouth flew open and a horrified frown drowned her smile. One teacher grabbed my hands to keep me from pulling out anything else and another teacher snatched the satchel up from the floor. By now the kids were laughing and screaming all at the same time. They seemed to enjoy the show.

Everything happened so fast. I was confused. I didn't understand what all the commotion was about. All I did was what the other kids had done, which was to find something in your house to show. I saw Pop with these things all the time.

Then Mrs. Kinney was yelling and screaming at me as she was dragging my little butt down the hall, gripping my arm so tightly it went numb, and, in her other hand, carrying the bag with my miniarsenal. I really did not understand what was going on.

"I didn't do nothin' wrong," I said over and over. "I didn't do nothin' wrong."

I sat in a chair with my arms folded, my feet swinging and a blank stare in my eyes. I waited outside the principal's office for an eternity before Pop came to get me. After that, I did not go back to school for a long time. I guess I had gotten myself suspended. Neither Ma nor Pop ever explained anything to me. Neither did Mrs. Kinney.

I was different from other kids. Something had to be wrong with me. People didn't like me for some reason.

I spent those days at home watching television and playing outside in the front yard.

When I went back to kindergarten, I didn't play with the other kids anymore. I didn't tease the girls. When I stood in the circle, I didn't sing "The Farmer in the Dell" or "Loopdy-Loo" anymore. And I definitely did not play Show and Tell. I would just sit there and stare. That was when I disappeared inside myself and barely spoke to anyone else but to me—in whispers and through my mind. I didn't talk to the other kids. I didn't talk to the teachers. That way, I figured I would never get into trouble again. I kept my personality and my creativity to myself. This way, I could have one kind of dream but live another kind of life.

Chapter Three

Daddy's Home

Who was he? I asked myself as this tough-talking, good-looking James Cagney type came to the house. It was late January, 1953. I was seven years old.

Andrew did not live with us anymore. Pop was already in his eighties and Ma was in her fifties; it probably became harder and harder to give Andrew the care he needed as he grew older. So he lived in a state institution for retarded kids in upstate New York.

I do not remember how or what I felt about his being away. I don't think I was especially happy about it. At least I had companionship with him. I don't even remember when I found out that Andrew was my brother. What was a brother? I had never heard the word before.

So there I was, this kid who didn't have a clue about da-da, and this man about five foot eight, well-built, with an attitude like Mr. Moore, comes into the house, acts as though I am completely invisible—I mean just as though I wasn't there. I was only too familiar with that scene. So what's new?

I remember Ma, myself and this man going together to Mount Calvary A.M.E. Church for the first time. Ma and I went almost every Sunday. This Sunday James went with us. I went to Sunday school first as I always did. I was doing everything but paying attention: wiggling in my seat, throwing paper balls across the room and trying to make the girls notice me (It's amazing the power females have over males, even at that age.).

I was still different. My clothes were clean but they were hand-me-downs: too big and old. Ma would always wear a hat and gloves, no matter if she had on a dress or a suit. She would wear her best jewelry—usually a brooch, necklace, matching earrings and bracelet. Her handbag and shoes always matched. James was one sharp dresser: two-toned shoes, a gangster-style hat, double-breasted suit and attitude for days. I would watch him out of the corner of my eye. I guess I noticed the attention Ma and James placed on their matching outfits and how little attention they placed on how I was dressed. But I didn't want to think too much about that. I'd rather think that they really cared about me and that the thing about the clothes wasn't really important.

When Sunday school was over I would go to the main sanctuary with the grown-ups and hear Reverend Hogan preach. I was in Junior Choir and sometimes we would sing. Ma was in the Senior Choir and on this particular Sunday it was their turn to sing. I sat in the middle row of pews. As the choir marched in, I saw James marching in with them.

Then church started and when it came time for the choir's first song, they all stood and James walked over to the piano, where soloists usually stood. I can still hear the ladies behind me whispering how he sounded like Nat King Cole. I sat still as his smooth, flawless voice resonated over our heads, bounced off the cathedral ceiling...hard to describe. He was electric. He'd hit those high notes over and over knowing how some of those women would respond; as though he was going for the knockout punch. Inevitably, some ladies would start shouting for the Holy Ghost and others would just faint. When he finished people were Amen-ing and Praise the Lord-ing and clapping. I was thinking, *Who is this man?*

He was the man I saw slap the sense out of his mother, Ma, every time he'd get drunk. He was the man who drank himself into violent, ugly rages that sent me running to hide. He was the man who had just come home from upstate New York:

Sing-Sing, to be exact.

He had been sent up in 1943 on charges of attempted robbery and first attempted grand larceny. So he was a thief. Andrew must have been one year old then. My mother was twenty-one. He was paroled June 17, 1946, a little more than two months before I was born. Then he did something to violate his parole and was sent back to Sing-Sing on August 23, 1949, to complete his term. I was three then, staying at Aunt Carly's. His release was delayed by seven days for bad time, but here it was 1953 and he was singing in church, his debt to society paid in full.

I don't remember when I started calling him Daddy. But he became Daddy to me. I wasn't invisible to him anymore: I was disgusting to him. I just tried to stay out of his way as much as possible, to avoid his unpredictable and unprovoked slaps and punches.

Ma was my refuge. She never yelled at me or raised her voice. Her tone was always even and gentle. She had no kisses or hugs for me—no one ever had—so I didn't know what I was missing. At least, not consciously.

Picture this: a pair of scuffed and run-over tan tie-up shoes at least two sizes too big for the feet wearing them. Big old baggy pants in doo-doo brown held up by frayed suspenders. These were my school clothes. This was also how I dressed for church. This was it. I was tall and skinny and I was in second grade wearing Pop's hand-me-downs.

I attended elementary school at PS 160. I hated school. In New York City "PS" stood for public school. I didn't get along with the other kids. When I passed them, they would laugh and nudge each other and sometimes shout at me. I would kick them or spit on them or curse them out or all of the above. I was a troubled kid looking for trouble.

No single incident stands out in my mind as much as the one that landed me in more than usual trouble. All these antics, the mean ones and the silly ones, derived from the same conclusion: Robert Beamon did not accept being invisible. So since I dressed like a clown and acted like a clown, there was just no way that I couldn't be seen.

At my house, things were happening about which I had no clue. One day, just like that, Ma and I moved from the house on Mathias Avenue and went to live in a bedroom in someone else's house.

We moved in with Saul and Iris Johnson. They spoke with accents. They were probably West Indians. They had four kids. Junior was one of the boys. He'd run around making buzz noises all the time. Reminded me of Andrew in a way, but without the seizures.

Saul made his living baking pies: apple and sweet potato. Saul would be in that kitchen for hours, baking up a storm. He sold his delicious pies to grocery stores and restaurants. You know how it smells when you pass by a Wonder Bread bakery? Just imagine having that aroma constantly in your house, where you sleep. Ma and I were cramped in that little room but that's not what I recall the most about being there.

They had rules in their house. Saul told me to play only in the front of the house. Of course, that went in one ear and out the other. I was running and cursing and whatever one afternoon all up and down the street, across the street, and around the corner.

Next thing I knew, Saul had stopped what he was doing to come get me from down the street. I tried to outrun him, but his legs were longer and faster than mine. When I got back to his house, he made me stand in the corner on one foot for what seemed an eternity but was only twenty minutes. I was punished a few more times even after that, and had to stand one-legged for twenty to thirty minutes, depending on the offense.

Saul was all right with me. I did not resent him nor did I fear him. I think he was probably the first man I ever respected. Sometimes, I would sit in the kitchen and watch Saul mix ingredients, make the crust, bake and pack his pies. Then he'd give me the bowl and I would use my finger to lick up all the sweet potato batter that was left. I would never help, no one would ever help him; not even Iris. Saul did everything by himself, from start to finish.

During the time we lived there, I only saw Daddy occasionally at church on Sundays. I never did find out why we moved from Mathias Avenue.

Ma was working as a domestic for various wealthy families in Manhattan and on Long Island. She told me once that she worked for the Barrymores, the famous family of actors. I do not know when Ma changed her life. I have been told that she used to own or manage a speakeasy on Long Island. She had a sister in Bridgeton, New Jersey, who had a back room in one of her clubs. So it would not be out of the question for Ma to have had an after-hours joint, too. At her sister's place, the back room was used for gambling: crap shooting, card playing, and numbers running.

One thing about Ma: playing her numbers was serious business—and she never missed a day. The numbers game was huge in New York. People would pay for their tuition, pay the rent, buy TVs and take trips with their winnings. People would dream about numbers and give tips on numbers. I think that's why Ma consulted that dream book every day.

Bumpy Johnson was the black numbers king of Harlem in the 1930s and 1940s, before Nicky Barnes. Bumpy was a legend to some blacks in New York. It was no secret that blacks started the lottery games in this country. The concept came from Africa. The numbers was a big cash business. First the Mob muscled in, now governments run the lotteries. Funny how time changes things.

The school thing was still not happening for me. I was truant all the time, from first grade on. I didn't know the alphabet and in third grade I could hardly write my name. The teachers would sometimes ask about homework and I'd show them addition and subtraction tables that I had copied from a book. I knew numbers better than words. My report cards were full of F's and Unsatisfactories.

My wardrobe still consisted of old worn-out clothes. The kids were still laughing at me. Come on, we all know just how cruel kids can be to one another, especially when one is wearing your grandfather's prewar, two-sizes-too-big clothes. I just wanted someone to notice *me,* the boy under those dreadful clothes. But it was too much to ask; the clothes were too much of a distraction.

I stayed in trouble. My neighborhood was full of scenes of violence, bloodstained sidewalks and stairwells, guns popping, stabbings, kids and adults dropping dead from drugs, bullets or knife wounds. A part of me was getting to the point where I wanted to stay away from all those negative forces out there. I was beginning to learn that the only way to survive in my house or outside my house was to be cool and not lose my temper. Another part of me had a very nasty temper and was always being loud, you know, calling attention to myself. But I began to notice that when I was quiet, people would leave me alone.

Ma and I left Saul and Iris and moved to South Jamaica Housing Projects. It was in the same neighborhood. When we got there, Pop and Daddy were there and so was a lady named Bert, short for Roberta. She was Daddy's girlfriend. I had seen her a couple of times before when she'd come to the other house. The five of us shared the two-bedroom apartment.

There were lots of kids living in the projects but none of them seemed to want to play with me. I was left out. They did not like me for some reason. I assured myself I didn't care.

I sank deeper and deeper into darkness. My stomach growled all the time. All I was eating was Cornflakes with water. Rarely did we have milk. I would steal boxes of Jujubes, candy bars, bags of potato chips, sodas and cookies from the stores. Once I'd get out the front door, I was gone— like lightning. I was that fast.

Every Tuesday and Thursday, I would stop by the Wonder

Bread thrift store where they sold day-old bread and bakery goods and swipe a quick meal. I'd steal food on my way there and on my way back from the Police Athletic League (PAL). I ran in the PAL track meets. I could run okay but I was hardly a standout. Although my group would win some local competitions, it was the other group that won the citywide ones. I was just there. It was some place to be.

Everybody in my world used the f-word; everything was a "f-ing this" and a "f-ing that"; shit and damn were like this and that in other people's vocabulary.

Bert looked at me and saw a punching bag. Daddy would drink and drink, curse and curse and when he beat her up she'd take out her frustrations on the punching bag. My little narrow butt would fly across the room from the impact of her fists. I was light as a feather. I guess my instinct told me not to hit her back. But then, I'd retaliate by busting some poor kid upside his head.

There was a woman, whose name I did not know, who was the neighborhood lush, always stoned. She wasn't that old, but she was always stumbling and staggering with a lit cigarette dangling from her mouth. She'd pick up men at the bar and have sex with them back in the alley, in the vestibule of any building or in a parked car. But sometimes she would tease the young boys on the block by raising up her skirt to show her naked butt, soliciting nickels, dimes and quarters. I was at the age when I was very curious about what was in my pants and what was under a girl's dress. I mean, I was the one who taped a compact-sized mirror to the top of my shoe so that I could see under the dresses of the girls when they came to the coatroom. Just goes to show you to what extent a boy will go "for a peek."

One day, a group of about five of us boys took her up on her offer. We had been contemplating "doing it" for weeks. I wasn't the first one to go and I wasn't the last. In a blink of an eye, I got erect, I penetrated her, thrust a few times amid cheering from the boys, and then it was all over. I was eight.

"It's Howdy Doody time. It's Howdy Doody time. It only cost a dime to get your booty shined," the kids would chime.

Television programs continued to enrapture me: *Howdy Doody, Father Knows Best* (a concept I could hardly relate to), *Dragnet, The Jackie Gleason Show* (and away we go!) and Art Linkletter's *People Are Funny*.

I was ten and growing up fast, but each year of life came and went without recognition. In my house my birthdays were never mentioned much less celebrated. So, I was different— and when you're different, you're different. For kids, it hurts to be different.

When I could get out, I would go to the community center in the projects. Mr. Robinson was the director there. Howie must have been his assistant. I'm not sure if I had fun there. I'm not sure if I knew what having fun was. But it was another place to go and there was always something to do there. I remember making a key chain once in arts and crafts class. But mostly I would play softball and, of course, basketball.

Even there I was always in trouble. Hitting, spitting, cursing—no social skills, no values, no discipline—a ten-year-old's way to process all that hurt. I guess I was sick and tired of being ignored, told to hush and pushed around.

And I kept getting suspended from school. At age eleven, I was assigned to counseling three times a week. I believe I went there for at least a year. It was at the Jewish Family Center. At first, Bert would take me there and wait for me. But after a while I would walk there by myself. It was on Jamaica Avenue, only a few blocks from my house.

My counselor was a woman named Mrs. Goodman. We had one-hour sessions. What stuck with me most about that experience is that she would sit with me and ask me what I thought about this and that. At first, it took me a while to respond because I had never been asked those things before. In my environment silence was golden, better for me to be quiet. Now I started to see how other people acted. I started to form opinions as to who I wanted to be. One thing I was clear about: I did not want to be like those people in my neighborhood. In counseling, I had to learn how to verbalize my feelings. Hell, I never consciously gave feelings any thought and, how do I say it? I didn't want to sound stupid. She wanted to know what I ate, what were my favorite toys, who were my friends and why. Deep stuff. Just finding the words to say what I thought was a trip. I mean, my vocabulary was limited to street talk or fragments of conversations I'd heard on television.

Mrs. Goodman was very patient with me. If I were a kid today, I'd probably be diagnosed with ADD, Attention Deficient Disorder, or be dismissed as having an MTV kind of attention span that only lasted two or three minutes at a time. All that sugar I was putting into my body contributed to my frenetic activity—all those JuJubees, sweet rolls and sugar water. I also had some very strong emotions that boiled deep down in my soul and they had no constructive outlet, no release. Nor did I have a "guide" to show me the path of least resistance.

Mrs. Goodman had something for me. She took out this contraption that had a long stem with a big horn on the end. She had my undivided attention as she spoke into this thing. Then she told me to say my name. I was shy and spoke very low.

"Robert Beamon," I said.

Then she played it back. I leaned back in my chair when I heard my voice say my name. So from that day on, I spoke into the dictaphone. Each day, talking would become easier and easier.

I felt comfortable there. I rarely missed a session and I was going there on my own. She would tell me that I was no different from anyone else. She would tell me that I was special, too.

Right. I was special. If this is what being special means, then God please make me something else! I cannot tell you how I processed that information or how I applied it. But I have to think that I must've filed it way back into my subconscious.

Because later, special would mean the same as different to me. Later, being different would be attractive to me. Because I would not want to fit in with the people around me.

Ozzie and Harriet, Leave It to Beaver and *The Ed Sullivan Show* were my favorite TV shows at that time. During those hours I would immerse myself in their world. In their world people acted differently: they were nice to one another, families were always having fun together and almost everyone was white. I wished that I had a family like that. I watched Ricky and David Nelson always having their father and mother there to talk to. The parents didn't punch on them or scream at them. They even sat down at the table together when they ate. They lived in a beautiful big house with trees and flowers outside. They had their own beds; even Ozzie and Harriet had separate beds. Hey, I was a kid. I didn't know any better.

The Cleavers were the same way, too. June and Ward Cleaver where always there for Beaver and Wally to talk to. Even when they got mad with them, they didn't call their kids "m-fs" (Remember, I'm talking about the 1950s.). When Beaver got in trouble, it would be about being late for school, or taking something of Wally's and then losing it, or walking off the curb with one foot in the street. His "trouble" and my "trouble" had very little in common.

Beulah was the only black person I saw on TV who had a show named after her. She played a live-in maid for a white family. She embarrassed me with her eyeball-rolling, headrag-wearing antics. Ma was a domestic and I never saw her act or dress like Beulah. She reminded me of Aunt Jemima on the pancake box, whom even my family criticized.

Earlier, I remember Kingfish and Sapphire's apartment on *The Amos and Andy Show*. It was small, but it was neat and nice. I remember the flowered drapes and the Priscillas (the sheer curtains in the middle of the drapes). But it wasn't anywhere near the houses of the Nelsons or the Cleavers. Andy lived in one room and Amos seemed always to be in his taxi.

Maybe he lived in his taxi. What did I know? I'd sit in front
of that small round screen and be swept into TV's black-and-
white wonderland for hours. I probably didn't even taste those
bowls of bland Cornflakes I was mindlessly shoveling into my
mouth.

There was one exception though. Nat King Cole. He had
his own show. It wasn't on long, but that's not how I measured
the impact that he had on a boy like me. He was dark brown,
just like me. He was a sharp dresser like Daddy, and I remember the women in the church saying Daddy sounded like Nat
King Cole when he sang. Cole's image is locked inside my
mind. He was a class act; sitting at a white grand piano, dressed
in a white dinner jacket with his hair slicked back. His velvet
voice and elegant image shared my living room for a few precious moments of time.

I slept in the same bed as Pop. Ma slept on the couch.
Daddy and Bert had the other bedroom to themselves. I slept
next to the window. The first time I heard the drums I thought
it was coming from the radio or I was dreaming or something.
It sounded like it came from *Ramar of the Jungle*. But then I'd
hear them most mornings. The sound was muffled, kind of
mystical and pure. The tones, the cadences, the rhythm sent
electricity through my body. Who was that? I looked out once
and saw an open window just across the courtyard.

Milford Graves must have been about thirteen then. He
was my introduction to percussion music. I was fascinated by
his drumming. I had never heard anyone play like that before—
and still haven't. Milford inspired me. Hearing him made me
want to play too. I was drawn in by the magnetism of the conga
tone. The rhythms distracted me. I heard them when I played
ball. I heard them when I walked. I turned up their volume in
my head when I wanted to drown out the sounds of chaos and
unhappiness, especially when Daddy went on his violent,
drunken binges. I would play on tabletops, car hoods, my
thighs—anywhere that had a beatable surface (except for Bert's

head).

That Christmas I got an Erector Set (building blocks), but my most coveted gift was a set of bongo drums—from Daddy.

* * *

Now I was in junior high, PS 40, Samuel Huntington School, named for the same man as the community center. Lord knows how I "graduated" from elementary school. I had a major discipline problem and I could not read or write.

What did I know about *Brown vs. Board of Education*, and Thurgood Marshall trying cases in the South, just so black kids could have the same education as white kids? What did I know about being forced to attend a school where all the books were old and worn-out? Where conditions were so bad that there were holes in the roof and no heat in the winter? What did I know about the NAACP fighting segregation in the schools? There I was going to school in New York City, one of the cultural capitals of the world, and I was being "promoted" for just being there—or not being there.

"Get your goddamn hands off me," I would yell at any grown-up except the ones at my house.

"I f—ed your mama last night," I would sneer in the face of any kid who looked like he was afraid of me.

"Want some of this romance in my pants?" I said to a girl in the coatroom. Then I exposed my penis to her. I was suspended again.

One time in school, I danced on the teacher's desk when she called my name for roll call. Of course I got in trouble again, but I did get noticed.

Another time during roll call, I saw that there was an empty seat next to a girl I liked. Nora was the most popular girl in my class. As the teacher was calling out the names, I leaned over to Nora and rapped a rhyme in her ear. It was meant to be a whisper but all those around us could hear:

I hate to talk about yo' Mama,
she's a good ol' soul.
She's got a tin can pussy and
a rubber asshole.
She's got hands on her titties
that can open the door.
Goddamn, the bitch is from
Baltimore!

Nora was not impressed by my performance. In fact, she was so annoyed that she pushed me away from her and told me to leave her alone. The other kids who heard me started laughing out loud. I got suspended again.

At home I was the designated babysitter. Daddy and Bert were married now and they started having children right away. When I came home about 3:15, Bert would leave for her job at the fish market across the street. Ma had moved to her own place in another building and Pop had died. I stayed with Daddy and Bert when they moved to a three-bedroom across the courtyard.

Christopher, my stepbrother, was born on Christmas Day and I stayed inside every day to take care of him. After Christopher, Bert had my stepsister Nanette and younger stepbrother Timothy. My job was to watch the children until Bert came home late at night. I would get lonely so I'd bang on the radiator pipes in the living room and yell "yo Mama" jokes to anybody who would listen.

"Bertie, Bertie, the fish lady. We can smell her all over the ocean." They would shout back to me through the pipes.

When I would hang out, I drank cheap wine and smoked cigarettes. I had to "step up to be a man:" I joined a gang. We called ourselves The Frenchmen. There were about fifteen to twenty of us, mostly from South Jamaica Housing Projects and mostly between the ages of twelve and fifteen. We fought with zip guns, chains and knives.

I saw a boy stabbed to death with an ice pick by a member of the Bricktown Chaplains. It was supposed to be only a fist-fight. But people fought dirty because to them cheating was cool.

I fought all the time and gained a reputation as a gang-banger. My fists were my weapons.

Then there was "Green Leaf Day"—an arbitrary holiday thought up by some older thugs as a scare tactic to intimidate the younger kids and to prove their manhood in front of the girls. Why? To have something to talk about.

They would declare Green Leaf Day without warning. A group of them would block the stairwells and the exit doors. Then they would ask you to show your green leaf. Of course, if you did not have one they would kick your butt.

They threw me up against the stairwell, kicked me in my ribs and punched me in my stomach. I knew they were out to get me—I had a reputation. I wouldn't fight back, there were too many of them and if I did they would be waiting for me in double numbers at three o'clock.

There were the thugs and then there was Duckie. He was in a class all by himself. We were about the same age. This brother was the sharpest dresser I had ever seen. At twelve or thirteen years old, Duckie was dealing in cocaine and heroin. He was the leader of a gang of dealers and thieves. He was always color-coordinated. If he wore green, then he would be wearing a pair of green silk pants, a green leather jacket, green silk shirt and green alligator shoes. He always had a big wad of money in his pocket. Always. I was very impressed with his clothes. In fact, I admired him.

When you live in the jungle, those whom one admires may end up being man-eating tigers. You live in an isolated world, surrounded by your own language, your own set of rules. So in my world, Duckie was an icon, *my* role model. He was clean, neat, smelled good, flashed expensive clothes and had cash.

Uh-huh, a role model for the stupid and ignorant.

It was around this time while I was hanging out on the corner doing nothing specific, when the cop cars came and surrounded the block. I was about to run when I heard, "Freeze. Put your hands up."

I had sense enough not to run and give them an excuse to shoot. Especially on that block—wasn't anything but scum and slime over there. They threw me in the car. Of course, when I got to the precinct, Detective White informed me that I looked like someone who had killed a man. Yeah, I was tripping while I was in there. But as soon as they released me, I was back on the streets, talking trash. The "boys" considered me a hero of some kind just because I had been taken into custody and was suspected of murder. It was a big deal.

I had a fight at school with Richard Abney. I forget what the fight was about but he tore my clothes and kicked me while I was down. That was called dirty fighting then and it demanded revenge. Today, that would be nothing. I was the new war counselor for The Frenchmen and I declared war on his butt.

In between classes, me and some of my boys went to his class and I knocked him out. One of the teacher's came in and tried to restrain me. I lunged directly at her and slammed her up against the blackboard. Pieces of chalk, erasers and chalk dust went flying everywhere. The kids were screaming and running—and my adrenaline was pumping.

Then a teacher from next door rushed to the room after hearing all the ruckus. When he spotted me with Miss So-and-So pinned up against the blackboard, he went ballistic. He yanked me off her, punched me in the face and knocked me down on the desk. Then he dragged me to the principal's office as I fought and cursed him every step of the way.

This time I was expelled. Big deal. What did I care? I headed straight for the basketball court and shot hoops with the other losers of the neighborhood. We were "cool" not to be in school. But it was more than that for me. You see, on the basketball court, it didn't matter what kind of clothes I had on, it didn't matter that I didn't know the alphabet. I knew how to count the score and how to count my money, but most of all I knew how to jump. I could jump higher than the older boys. Even when I was in elementary school, everybody always wanted me on their team. It was there, on the court—in the streets, that I began to feel as though I was a part of something.

When I came home, Bert yelled something before I even got into the house. Then she slapped me. I came "that close" to hitting her back, but this time it was different. She could tell by the look in my eyes that I could hurt her. I was tired of being mistreated by her. I knew she was going to tell Daddy. So I ran away with just the clothes on my back. It was the dead of winter.

I knew a boy, Freddie, who told me that I could stay with him. When I got to his house, I was shocked. At least where I lived the glass was in the windows and we had some heat. Freddie, his girl with a baby and some other folks lived in the condemned building. It was colder in there than it was outside. The baby was running around in a filthy dress with bowels packed in her gray diaper and her nose running. The whole place reeked of urine. Big cockroaches were crawling everywhere. Jesus! I had jumped from the skillet into the fire, but I was not turning back. Hell, I was expelled from school anyway.

I slept with my coat on for seven days, hardly ate and had not had a bath since I left home. I couldn't take it anymore. As much as I hated to, I went back to the house. Daddy and Bert had filed a missing person report with the police. I think they were relieved that I was okay. Then Ma came and took me over to her place. She had been looking for me. I had to appear in juvenile court the next day or they'd have a warrant out for me. I was on my way.

The word out on the street was that I was getting ready to be sent upstate. Translation: I was getting ready to be locked up.

Chapter Four

Someone to Watch Over Me

We were the first ones there. I sat next to Ma in the front row waiting for the judge to call my name. I was a tough one, after all I had been suspected of murder once. I was the war counselor for The Frenchmen. Couldn't tell me nothing! I was the basketball star of the neighborhood. I smoked, I drank, I sold a little marijuana mixed with tealeaves. I had one of the foulest mouths on the block. I sang backup during street corner doo-wop sessions. I was a musician-in-training. I couldn't read the front of a newspaper. I couldn't write a decent sentence. I thought it was nothing to steal. After all, Daddy was a convicted thief and I saw Bert shoplift some clothes once. Everyone I knew stole. So what was the big deal?

It didn't bother me to get "physical" with anyone, either. Come on, I spent most of my life defending myself from thugs who punched me upside my head for recreation. Bert and Daddy knocked me around way beyond what discipline called for. I had never been hugged or kissed or touched with affection. So what the hell did I care about sitting in this damn courtroom, looking at this old white man dressed in a black choir robe? In my mind, I was already serving time.

Ma, on the other hand, didn't feel that way. I sat tight-lipped next to her. She clutched a delicate linen-and-lace hankie in one hand. Her eyes would well up with tears every now and then.

I pretended not to notice the procession of young teenage boys, handcuffed and somber-faced, who marched in front of the judge. The judge was pounding his gavel one case after another; sending one young thug after another upstate without batting an eye.

"Robert Alfred Beamon," the bailiff called.

Ma immediately stood up but I took my time.

"Robert Beamon, why is it that you cannot stay in school?" the judge asked.

"I don't know—the teachers kept putting me out," I said, as I shrugged my shoulders and shifted my eyes to the floor like I was some kind of idiot.

"Look at me when I speak to you, Mr. Beamon," the judge demanded.

Then my grandmother started to speak. She convinced the judge that she would be one hundred percent responsible for me, if only he would not send me upstate. The judge seemed reluctant, but finally said, "Robert Beamon, you are very lucky to have a grandmother like Bessie Beamon." He flipped through page after page of my file, then he paused for what seemed forever.

"Mrs. Beamon, I'm going to take a chance on you. Since you believe in your grandson that much—I'm going to give him another chance—his last chance."

Then he paused and glared directly into my eyeballs.

"You're going to a 600 school, Robert. There, if you are really serious about doing something with your life, you'll have an opportunity to do so. But I admonish you, Robert Beamon—look at me—if I ever see you in my courtroom again, I am sending you upstate, on the first thing smoking." He spoke quietly, his eyes creating a kind of deadlock with mine. My instincts told me he meant business.

Seemed like all that business Mrs. Goodman told me about being "special" had come to pass, in a way. All the "boys" were expecting me to end up upstate, enrolled in one of the prep schools for Sing-Sing or Riker's Island. I was stupid enough then not to even be scared.

My grandmother just broke down and sobbed. I didn't realize it then, but she probably didn't want to see me end up like Daddy. This was a wake-up call for her. For me? Are you kidding? I was still sound asleep.

I've seen kids today who act like that. You know the ones. Just try to start a conversation with one:

"What did you do in school today?"

"Nuthin'"

"What is your favorite color?"

"I don't know."

"What do you want to be when you grow up?"

"I don't know."

Like pulling teeth, isn't it? Well, I was worse than that. I was so caught up in day-to-day living that I could survive but I couldn't thrive. I didn't know how.

When we left court, it was a long subway ride back. Ma was visibly shaken. Tears streamed uncontrollably down her cheeks, but she did not sob. She did not speak. I had never seen her so broken before. It was like something had just knocked the wind out of her. Though I did not think much of the entire scenario, I did not want to subject her to anything like that again.

We went home. I was relieved to live alone with Ma. It was best. I couldn't stay with Bert. She was eventually going to provoke me to knock the hell out of her one day. I think the trouble between me and Bert was that every time she looked at me she thought of my mother. In her mind, I was another set of baggage to her marriage with Daddy.

Plus, Daddy had been away for about a year. I heard that he had been accused of raping a thirteen-year-old girl one night after he played cards with her parents. It happened the night before I was going to ask the girl's older sister to be my girl-friend. They lived in the next building. Her mother and father and Daddy drank all the time; they were always drunk. When they'd get together, they'd play cards and drink whiskey all night long. Inevitably, a fight would erupt over who played what, who cheated, etc. etc. It was the same old, same old. The details are fuzzy. Though I remember Daddy resurfaced the summer before I started going to the 600 school.

In the New York City public school system of numbers, PS 600 meant "alternative" or a last-chance place to send incorrigible youths before they were locked up. It was located in Manhattan on Fifty-second and Broadway. I took the F train from Queens to get there.

To keep myself occupied during the daily ride there, I would carry a song in my head—humming or singing it as we traveled under the East River into Manhattan. They played that song, "You Talk Too Much" over and over on the radio. Even though I thought it was corny, I found myself singing it anyway.

When I walked up from the subway, I saw the famous Cheetah Club, a cabaret where the likes of Duke Ellington, Ella Fitzgerald and Frank Sinatra used to perform. Across the street from this fabulous club stood PS 600, a dark brown, ordinary prewar building. There were cage bars on the windows: such a peculiar look to be smack dab in the middle of the Great White Way. I was fourteen. It was 1960 and a five-room apartment on Sixty-fifth and Park Avenue rented for $500 a month. Can you imagine? Or if you wanted to live on the West Side, how about $425 for an eight-room apartment with a view? Today those same apartments might be anywhere between $3,000 to $6,500 a month.

Now it was quiet inside my head as I walked in through the main entrance: no songs, no thoughts of entertainers, females or fashion statements. There was a man in the entrance hall who, upon seeing me, instantly directed me to go to the office, one door down. The mood was very no-nonsense; the man in the office was polite but you understood that nonsense would not be tolerated. He told me to report immediately to Room 203.

"When the bell rings, you must be in your seat. If you are not, then you will be held for detention and issued the appropriate number of demerits. If you get a certain number of demerits, you go back to the judge. Got it?" he said.

I nodded.

"What did you say?" he asked.

"Yes, I got it," I responded.

"Yes, what, Mr. Beamon?" he demanded.

"Yes, sir," I said.

Things were different already and I been there less than five minutes. I found myself fast-walking to Room 203. As I approached the classroom, I saw the silhouette of a tall, muscle-bound man, whose build resembled that of a NFL linebacker, standing at the door. The halls were dimly lit and as I approached his features took shape. He stood there greeting every boy who entered the room. When I came in, he put his hand on my shoulder and asked my name.

"Robert Beamon," I mumbled.

"Robert Beamon, my name is Mr. Jones and from now on when I ask you a question, I expect you to speak up with your head up," he said. "What's your name?" he repeated the question.

"Robert Beamon," I answered in a clear voice with my head up.

"Okay, I want you to sit right there," he said, pointing to a center seat in the second row.

Man, oh man. What was this, I wondered? I walked to my seat, didn't look at anybody, and sat my butt down.

When Mr. Jones closed the door, I was sitting among other thugs and wannabe gangsters from the Bronx, Brooklyn, Harlem, Manhattan and Queens. There were fifteen of us, all about the same age, fourteen or fifteen years old. There were five Hispanics and ten Blacks.

"My name is Mr. Jones. I am a certified blackbelt in karate, like all of your teachers. We do not play games here.

We can crack your skull wide open with a single chop. Order is the name of the game here—and we will keep it by any means necessary. Understand?"

"Yes, Mr. Jones," we all said in unison, nodding our heads.

Thank God, Daddy had a fleeting moment of compassion when he taught me how to read. It was only a few months back. He said he had gotten tired of me bringing home all those F's. He then commanded me to sit down and read the sports page out loud.

The headline read: RAFER JOHNSON WINS GOLD IN ROME. I struggled over the six words like I was asked to read Japanese. Daddy shook his head and told me how pitiful I was and how sick he was of it. So he sat down and went over each word with me. He showed me how to pronounce vowels and how to figure out the words phonetically. Every day, I was to follow his instruction. It wasn't hard to do because another world then opened up for me. And, of course, knowing how to read lifted a giant burden off my shoulders. I never realized what a difference it made to read until I was able to do it.

In six weeks, I was reading—still struggling over the words—but reading just the same.

So by the time I went to PS 600, I could at least read, if only on a remedial level. Thank God. Who knows, they may have given me detention and demerits for not knowing how to read.

For the first time in my life I was learning something in school. There were disruptions, but it was clear that if you disrupted you were out. But things were far from perfect. I had one problem I didn't know how to resolve without jeopardizing my future. The rules of "the street" demanded I not continue to let this happen without dealing with it head on. So I came to school on a mission one day.

Howard was a seventeen-year-old sexual pervert, a rapist. There were times when he would pass me in the hall and intentionally rub his body against mine. Other times, he would loud-talk me in front of some other boys about me being his "bitch" and how good his "dick" would feel in my "ass".

It was no secret that Howard had "turned out" several other boys. I wondered how he could get away with it with all the security we had. But if it could happen in "the joint" every day, I guess it could certainly happen here.

Finally, I'd had enough. If I didn't do something quick, I figured this pervert was going to rape me. I had to fight him and win, or else I would be raped and labeled "a bitch" forever.

The day I decided to take a stand, I sat in math and tried to focus on fractions, but I was anticipating my attack on Howard during lunch period. I was ready to take the consequences in order to save my dignity.

The bell rang for lunch and I walked alone to the cafeteria. The menu was my favorite: cheeseburgers and french fries, but I had no appetite.

Howard was waiting for me—standing in the aisle where I had to pass. I walked toward him carrying my tray of food. As I passed him, Howard pinched me on the butt. I spun around and shoved my tray into his face as hard as I could. Then I wrapped my arms around this scum's legs, threw him on the table and beat the living shit out of him with a flurry of iron-clad-like punches to his face and body.

It took Mr. Jones and two other teachers to pull me off him. I just knew I had blown it. But what choice did I have? To be raped and God knows what else? But after they separated us, they simply told us to cool out. Nothing else was said. They must have realized what I was up against with this guy. Howard left me alone from that day on. That's how it is in the streets—you have to kick ass to gain respect or be regarded as a "poo-butt."

What are you doing here? I asked myself. *You don't belong here.*

I no longer had anything in common with those guys. I kept to myself and observed the situations and the people around me. I remember consciously saying to myself, "I do not want to be like them," or "I do not want to end up like him." I didn't want to go home either. I just didn't feel like I belonged anywhere. I guess that is why it was a blessing to have met Bra. The timing could not have been more perfect.

* * *

Walter Patterson attended St. Agnes, a Catholic school. His nickname, Bra, had nothing to do with a brassiere. He was different from everyone else in the neighborhood because he'd go to school dressed the same every day. He wore a white shirt with a starched collar, navy blue bow tie, dark pants and spit-shined black leather shoes.

I'd met him before. We shared a love for the congas. He played his congas sometimes in the courtyard and was pretty good. Anyway, I was on my way to Mrs. Moore's candy store—couldn't leave that sugar alone—when I saw Bra.

"Still playing?" he asked.

"Naw, not much. What about you?"

"I practice every day after school. You should come by and we'll practice together," Bra said.

I told him that I'd be over in a little while, as soon as I left Mrs. Moore's. But once I got to the store, I saw some of the "boys" who were playing records on the jukebox, especially a singing group, Shep and the Limelites who were from Queens. Although we had worn out their hit song, "Daddy's Home," on the jukebox, we never passed up an opportunity to harmonize with the record when we were together. So there I was trying hard to fit in with these guys while at the same time feeling like I didn't belong there, either. However, it was our routine and it had become a familiar habit.

The time passed and I forgot all about Bra's invitation. I didn't get a chance to hang with The Frenchmen much anymore since I started going to school in Manhattan. I had started to feel different. I had a responsibility to myself now. I had homework and if I did not follow the rules there, I was going to jail. Ma finally bought me some nice clothes on credit from Berger Brothers. Duckie could still outdress me but, for the first time in my life, I had on clothes that were brand new, my taste and my size.

In class, I would struggle with English grammar. But I kept trying, I was not discouraged. At that school, you were not looked down upon if you made a mistake. As long as you made the effort to improve, that was what was important. I didn't have any running buddies to speak of. I pretty much kept to myself. Since I kicked Howard's ass, no one bothered me and I bothered no one.

I had two gym teachers, Mr. Rothenberg and Mr. Rogers, both of whom were Jewish. Rothenberg was white. Rogers was black. It was the first time I'd ever seen a black man wear a yarmulke.

Rothenberg was short but built like a Mr. Olympus or something. Rogers, on the other hand, was about five foot ten, slim and built like a long-distance runner. They would always tell me that I had real talent.

"You know, Beamon, if I could play like you, I wouldn't be doing it here in a 600 school," Rothenberg would say.

"You really got something going for you, Beamon," Rogers would say.

I loved playing basketball. We'd play other teams in the school. I'd play center, Bugs would play guard, Tony would play guard and Freddie would play forward. They were probably a year or so older than me. Bugs was one of those untouchable-type gangbangers from Manhattan but he was cool with me. Tony Rodriquez was a black Puerto Rican from Manhattan and a good, solid ballplayer. Then there was Freddie Meyers. He was the business partner of Pee Wee Kirkland, one of the biggest drug dealers in Harlem—and "he could play him some basketball."

There I was a star. The star athlete of PS 600. A dubious honor, huh?

There was no question that I started to feel differently about myself. First of all, I knew I didn't belong there with those other boys. I didn't think like them. Yeah, I could curse and talk crap the same, but there was something else going on with me that I could not define. Now that I could read and write, I didn't hate school, even a 600 school. Now that I had decent clothes to wear, I didn't hate going to school, even a 600 school.

Having decent clothes to wear made a big difference in my life. I did not perceive myself as a clown or as a person undeserving of having clothes that fit anymore. I had a lot of confusion in my heart as to why my grandmother never bought decent clothes for me until I went to a 600 school. Did the teachers say something to her? I'll never know for sure.

Even my after-school behavior changed. After school, instead of going to Ma's, I'd go straight to Bra's house.

Mrs. Patterson, Bra's mother, was an attractive woman in her thirties. She was attractive to me not so much because of her looks but mainly for the way she ran her household. She was a good-hearted person and was very clear about how to raise her family. She was a single parent, a strong individual who took pride in her children. She made sure that Bra and his sisters always had a hot dinner. Her children had great manners and a lot of respect for her. She worked and even though the odds may have been against her, having to raise three children alone, she took great care of them—emotionally, spiritually and physically.

I remember the first time I came to their house like it was yesterday. When I knocked on the door, the eldest girl, Tisha, answered. I guess she was about twelve then. She invited me in and showed me to the small, spotless kitchen where Bra was sitting at the table working on his homework.

"Bobby, man, what a surprise. I didn't know what had happened to you," Bra said.

"Oh, man, it takes me a while sometimes," I said. "But, hey, you're doing your homework, I can come back later."

"No, no, no. I was just finishing up. You're just in time for conga practice," he said as he closed his book.

Then I followed him into the bedroom where his set of congas stood in the corner. We sat on the bed and he rolled one drum over to me and we just started jamming. Time just stood still. More than an hour passed and I hadn't realized it. Then we heard the front door open.

Bra immediately stood up and motioned for me to follow him. I walked behind him to the living room.

"Bobby, this is my mother, Mrs. Patterson," he said as he walked over and kissed her.

"Hello, Mrs. Patterson," I said to the woman in the white nurse's aide uniform.

She seemed to be very pleasant with a warm disposition. Then Bra's sisters, Tisha and the younger one came up and hugged her even before she could put her purse down on the table. It was really nice to see that.

"Bobby, are you going to stay and have dinner with us?" she asked with a smile.

"Yes, he is, Mommy," Bra answered for me before I could speak.

Then she went into the kitchen, the girls went to the back and Bra and I played and talked until dinner was ready. They were so pleasant to be around.

I was always so hungry. It was so seldom that I ate a hot dinner. At least at school, I had a decent lunch. No more Cornflakes and water for breakfast, lunch and dinner. That stopped after I moved in with Ma. Although there was food in the fridge, she was never there for dinner. In fact, I wouldn't see Ma until the morning when she was on her way to work.

So that was my beginning with the Patterson family. Every day for almost a year I would go by straight from school, do my homework when Bra did his, practice drums, watch TV and become a permanent fixture at their dinner table. There was rarely a night when I would leave before 11:00 P.M.

It felt very natural to be there. And you know what else? In a way, I looked forward to the daily subway rides on the F train. I was really beginning to open up my senses to the world. I would read the backs of newspapers and books held by people whose faces were buried in the words.

There is an unspoken rule for subway riders, "Never look anyone in the eyes." But I would—all the time. I would observe the women in business clothes—how their hair would bounce; how their sweet or spicy fragrances would massage the thick air. I would pan the car with my eyes, and admire the neatly dressed men with clean fingernails and freshly polished shoes. Riding the train was an education. One thing about New Yorkers who take public transportation, they are always reading something and, when asked, have a definite opinion about world and local politics.

I became more and more uncomfortable at the 600 school. I now knew for certain that I did not belong there—even when I won the in-school track-and-field meet in my second year. That day, I won the 100 meters, fifty meters, 200 meters and the long jump. My athletic stardom was etched in stone there. Both Rothenberg and Rogers kept reaffirming to me that I really had something "special" going for me. There was that word again. It was like they were trying to tell me something.

Meanwhile, my musical skills were becoming sharper and sharper. Bra had a portable hi-fi in his room. We would play along with the salsa records of Eddie and Charlie Palmieri, Mongo Santamaria, Tito Puente and Olatunde. The tonal combinations from Afro-Cuban, West African and Puerto Rican rhythms would shoot through my body and down to my hands. Each placement of the palm of the hands and fingers on the drum meant something: ancient language played out on animal hides that mimicked the beat of the heart. We would study their polyrhythmic techniques—which took years to perfect—and marvel at their musical skills. We would jam to a clave beat, which sounded like the beginning beat from Bo Diddley's "A Gun Slinger." Latin music made me go crazy. It could have taken the place of the blood in my veins. Milford Graves introduced me to percussion music, and in New York City, percussion was king at the time. Bra and I were alike in that sense: we were both captivated by percussion music. We were glued together with that passion. I literally lived with the Pattersons. I only slept at Ma's. For a moment I had a taste of *Ozzie and Harriet*—minus Ozzie and with a conga beat.

Ma did not like me spending so much time at Bra's house. So she told Daddy to go over there and see what was going on. I remember hearing this faint knock at the door. Bra asked who it was. When Daddy answered, I was surprised.

Mrs. Patterson was in the kitchen preparing dinner and came out to greet him. She wore a flowered apron over her clothes. She was about five foot four, nice figure, delicate features and her hair was cut close to her head in a pixie cut. It looked great on her.

My heart was caught in my throat anticipating the worst. She invited Daddy to stay for dinner and he accepted. I was relieved. Bra and I went back to his room and started playing again, while Daddy sat in the kitchen with Mrs. Patterson.

The dinner must have gone well, because now it was me and Daddy spending our evenings with the Pattersons. Daddy had become a regular dinner guest and soon ended up in her bedroom. I could see the handwriting on the wall.

At first, everything was fine. Mayberry was a long way from Queens. But still, I could escape and relate to the simplistic lives of Sheriff Andy Taylor, Barney Fife, Aunt Bea and especially Opie.

Bra and I would watch my old favorites together: *Ozzie and Harriet* and *Leave It to Beaver*. But now I had a crush on Eve Arden, *Our Miss Brooks*. The Pattersons were the closest thing to my dream of having a family like I saw on TV.

Ma was not happy about Daddy sleeping with Mrs. Patterson. He was married, after all. He and Bert lived right there in the next building. Plus, he had three little mouths to feed. It wasn't long before Daddy and Mrs. Patterson started to have arguments. It was the first time I'd heard any anger expressed in their home. Then Daddy stopped coming over. I continued to go but things were not the same. They never treated me any differently; I just felt awkward about the situation.

I kept thinking about how it would be to go to regular school.

I thought about the last time I saw Duckie. He was sick; vomiting all over his matching silk pants and shirt. He had started to consume his own product. He became his own biggest customer, shooting tiny bags of heroin into his veins. I watched with disgust as Duckie, the guy I used to admire, walked around like a zombie and slumped into a catatonic stupor. I didn't know a lot of things, but I knew I didn't want to be like him.

I thought about some of The Frenchmen. They were either sitting around drinking cheap wine and smoking dope, hanging out in the streets all day looking for someone to rob or pick a fight with, getting chased down by the law or getting shot down or stabbed and left on the streets to die. I knew I didn't want to be like them, either.

I didn't want to end up like those trifling losers who raised hell and spent all their paychecks at the neighborhood bar that was known as The Bucket of Blood. Every weekend those country-ass fools would shoot and stab one another to the blues of Muddy Waters playing on the jukebox.

Every payday, Bert would go to Daddy's construction site and wait for him. She had to make sure she'd get the money for food and bills before Daddy would blow it all on whiskey and women. I didn't want to be like that.

Nor, did I want to blow an opportunity like Daddy did a

couple of years ago with this big record producer.

Daddy was truly a Dr. Jekyll and Mr. Hyde. Between his jail time and his drunken rages, he performed now and then with a local singing group. They would let him sing whenever he showed up. They couldn't depend on him to be a regular member of the group, but he had "the chops" and he had "a thing" with the ladies.

I think the man's name was Moses. Moses heard Daddy one night and was so impressed that he offered to set up a recording session at his studio. He told Daddy that he would cut a record on him and was positive that he could get it played on the radio. So Daddy agreed to do it.

Two hours before the recording session at Moses' studio, Daddy went on a whiskey binge that lasted until the next morning. Moses was furious. When he found Daddy at home, there was a lot of finger-pointing and yelling. Moses came that close to punching Daddy out.

Daddy had a God-given talent with his voice. Here he had an opportunity to cultivate it. I'm sure that the reason Moses walked away and didn't look back was simply that there were many other talented people out there but not every talented person has the discipline and the commitment to excel. That's the difference. Moses probably felt that if Daddy would sabotage himself then surely he would not hesitate to sabotage Moses and his company. I was not going to be like that.

I had lots of teachers who taught me how not to do things. I had lots of role models who I didn't want to be like.

There was a man who lived in the neighborhood—not the projects—who seemed special to me. Frenchy was about six foot five and had a bald head. He looked like a genie without the earring. I only remember seeing him when the weather was warm. He would wear shorts and sandals—that Greenwich Village look. I guess I remember him so well because he stood out; he was different and I liked that. He didn't look or act like the other people I knew in my neighborhood. He made a big impression on me. He would walk the streets tall and straight with his two Great Danes. I had never seen dogs that grand. They were a sight to see. I thought Frenchy was the coolest man. I wanted to have dogs like those.

When I'd pass by Frenchy's house, I could hear the mambo music playing inside. People affectionately called Frenchy "The Mambo King" because he loved to dance the mambo and rumba—and danced them so well. I would sometimes stop and watch his Great Danes in the front yard and tell myself that one day I'd have dogs like that.

The only pet I remember having as a kid was a little white dog named Snowball. I only had him for a couple of months when we lived on Mathias Avenue. Then one day, I found Snowball in the yard with white suds bubbling from his mouth. Just when I was about to run over and pick him up, Ma screamed from the window for me not to touch him. Snowball had been infected with rabies.

*   *   *

It was late spring of 1962; I was fifteen going on sixteen. I stood about six foot even; I was slim and muscular. Posters announcing the Junior Olympics were plastered all over the place: on boarded-up buildings, on light poles, on buses and in subways. When I saw those signs something in my body reacted. It was like some kind of inner urging that made me want to do something. It almost felt like a push.

I remembered what Mr. Rothenberg and Mr. Rogers told me. I decided that I needed an opportunity to take myself to another level of sports and compete. I didn't have any spikes and I didn't have subway fare to get to the competitions. I remembered that a boy at the community center did have spikes and I asked him if I could borrow his. But when the time came, the boy was nowhere to be found.

Junebug and Roy, whom I knew from PAL, were competing, too, so we planned to go together. Randall's Island was a one-hour trip. I asked Ma and Daddy for sixty cents for subway and bus fare. They didn't have it. It was just short of an hour to make an hour trip. So I took what they had and knocked door-to-door in my building and collected the rest.

We were so lucky. We were cutting it so close. As soon as we got to the station, the subway was waiting. Then when we got to the bus, it was a block away. We made it fifteen minutes before the long jump was to start.

I did not have a coach nor was I represented by a sports program. I asked a boy I had never seen before if I could borrow his shoes to jump in. He said no. I asked another boy and his father said no. But I was determined. I was going to ask until someone said yes—and finally someone did.

It was a clear day, not a cloud in the sky. It was so blue and I felt so free, so unrestricted. When my name was called, I didn't even think about anything. I walked to the runway, composed myself for a moment and then sprinted down the runway and took off at the board.

When I landed I had broken the Junior Olympics long jump record. People probably wondered who I was and where I came from as I stood at the victory podium with the gold medal dangling from my neck. I couldn't have answered that—I didn't know myself.

The next morning on the front page of *The Daily Mirror* sports section were the results of the Yankees game. But there in the middle of the page was a huge photograph of me jumping, under a headline that read, BEAMON JUMPS 24'1" IN JUNIOR OLYMPICS. I could not believe my eyes. It was me! Me! I wasn't in the newspaper for shooting someone or going to jail or overdosing. I was in the newspaper for doing something good. I could not believe my eyes.

Ma said, "That's nice."

Daddy said, "That's nice."

Bert said, "Oh, that's nice."

But their nonchalant attitude did not burst my bubble. I was proud of myself. Not stuck on myself but just proud. I felt light—the weight of doubt and fear had disappeared. I wanted to fly; I wanted to see how high I could go.

I would turn sixteen that August. My mind was made up.

"Daddy, I want to go ‚to regular school. I want to go to Jamaica High School. Can you help me?" I had never asked him for anything before.

Daddy told me that he would take The Daily Mirror article to track coach Larry Ellis at Jamaica High School, and he kept his word. Coach Ellis was interested.

Mr. Louis Schuker, the principal at Jamaica High, had a long talk with me and Coach Ellis. He said that the odds of a 600 school student making it in a regular school environment were next to zero. His admonition to me was reminiscent of the one given by the judge who had sentenced me to the 600 school.

"Beamon, any trouble out of you—and you are out of here," Mr. Schuker said. "Do I make myself clear?"

"Yes, sir," I answered firmly and clearly.

I knew that I wasn't going anywhere but Jamaica High. *This* was were I wanted to be. *This* was were I belonged.

Chapter Five

Walk Like a Man

Bobby Beamon had arrived.

In current events class we discussed the Freedom Riders. Our assignments included watching the news and reading newspapers like *The New York Times, New York Daily Mirror*, and magazines like *Life* and *Time*. Then we would have a discussion. I never thought of the concept of segregation, let alone separate but equal, until then. Places like Mississippi, South Carolina and Alabama seemed like light-years away from me.

On television I saw the Freedom Riders. They were mostly young college students, black and white, many of them from New York. I remember seeing them sitting peacefully at a lunch counter waiting to be served, and mean-looking rednecks taunting them, hitting them and even spitting on them. I could never have made it with nonviolence. I would have knocked out somebody's lights.

I remember those black-and-white images telecast on the evening news from the streets of Birmingham, Alabama. They were horrible. I remember those huge German shepherd attack dogs with their fangs exposed, lunging at peaceful marchers: men, women and children in Ingram Park. The pictures of those dogs stuck in my mind. They were like vampires, possessed by some evil force as were the policemen who sicced them on those defenseless people. I saw those demons beat unarmed demonstrators with billy clubs, spray them with high-powered fire hoses until they fell. It looked worse than any gang fight I had ever seen. And then there was George Wallace, the governor of Alabama, whose demonic leadership milked the violent, sick and despicable behavior. That is when I learned about the Ku Klux Klan, the cowards who hid behind white hoods and robes in their proclaimed honor of dead Confederate soldiers. Now, just how damn sick can you get? All of this racial stuff left me confused. But I knew one thing: I wasn't going anywhere south of New York City.

The bell would always interrupt some spirited discussion we would have in current events. Most of us would sigh, because we weren't ready to end it yet.

I felt like that about long jumping and basketball, too. Larry Ellis was my track and field coach. Hilton "Hilty" Shapiro was my basketball coach. After school, I was either in practice or traveling to a competition. Sports demanded most of my time and cut short my time with Bra. We were still friends but I no longer had the time nor the inclination to go there after school. What we had shared satisfied both our senses at the time. His family had become a surrogate family to me, filling up a gigantic void in my life when I needed it most. I had become his musical brother, who shared his love of percussion music and the ability to play it.

My interest in music did not falter. Sometimes, I would play congas for the dance classes at Bernice Johnson's Dance School. Riley Hall, who played with Milford Graves, would play there, too. I would watch him and listen to his interpretations on his drums. I bet he and Milford had no idea of the positive influence they had on me. Sometimes we inspire others by just doing what we do well.

I was also playing trap drums. But I had a gnawing appetite to learn more, musically. So I took up trombone and played in the school band. I sat in the second row of the brass section. I had a tendency to accidentally hit Ricky with the slide. Poor Ricky sat in front of me. Also, my pitches were noticeably off-key. Then one day at practice, Ricky shouted "ouch" one time too many and trombone number three in the second row was flat one time too many. Mr. Michaels, the band director, lost his cool and patience.

"Bobby Beamon, get out of here and go to the dean's office," said Mr. Michaels.

"Was it *that* bad?" I asked.

"It was worse than that," he said.

The class chuckled. I had a reputation for being funny. I knew I should have practiced. I went to the dean's office and he officially took me out of band. Thus, the end of my trombone career.

I wasn't afraid of going to the dean's office or the principal's office anymore. I was in synch with people. I wasn't being misunderstood, I wasn't being stupid. I did get the hell scared out of me early on, though. I had only been at Jamaica High for a couple of weeks. I walked into the building with my hat on, which was a no-no. I didn't do it on purpose—just hadn't gotten adjusted to the rules yet. And who do I walk right into? Mr. Schuker.

I immediately realized the hat was on my head and snatched it off. Well, I just knew he was going to send me back to the 600. He didn't even mention it. Thank God! That was the last time I wore my hat inside Jamaica High.

I know what you're thinking: Things have really changed, haven't they?

Guess what? I wasn't invisible anymore. People saw me.

It was 1963, my seventeenth year. Although I was chronologically older than the average sophomore, who was fifteen, I was not more mature. So, I fit in perfectly. I no longer asked myself, "What am I doing here?" I belonged just where I was.

I snuggled into my new life and found it warm and cozy. Yeah, a former war counselor "snuggled." I cannot think of a better word to describe it. Except at those times when I feared that it was all a dream; that I'd wake up and find myself back at

Freddie's, sleeping on the floor in my coat with cockroaches running across my face and the winter's cold nipping at my butt. Or Bert slapping me from my sleep, yelling at me to go to the kitchen and wash the plate that she just finished using. Or Daddy knocking me to the ground for being in his sight when he didn't want to see me.

Instead of warm and cozy, the chilly heaviness of anxiety would invade my soul. Like sitting by a warm, soothing, crackling fire, and suddenly an icy wind pushes open the door and blows out the fire. And there you are, left shivering and frightened by the abrupt transition from peace to panic, from warmth to cold. But just as quickly as those thoughts would come, I'd experience a sensation of weightlessness as if some invisible force was plowing through and demolishing all my doubts and fears. This scenario repeated itself hundreds of times. I was so nervous that my dream wouldn't last—so afraid that it was merely an illusion.

* * *

I loved being an athlete. I just wanted to train hard and do something special with my life.

"I can only show you the way," Coach Ellis would say. "It's up to you to go there."

During this time, I seemed to hear my mother's words quite often. "My son, he will be someone special..." she had told Ma.

Ma had opened an account for me at Berger Brothers, a department store in Queens. I had no idea why Ma had money now. Now I wore leather loafers, button-down shirts and a Brooks Brothers-type houndstooth cap. I dressed like an Ivy Leaguer.

I'd buy three pairs of black pants and several sweaters and shirts and rotate them over and over. I was no fashion plate, but I was always clean, pressed and well groomed—and it didn't hurt that I was tall and slender.

Her name was Janet. She seemed to know something about everything. We would talk for hours—walking down the street, in the park, on the stoop. I did not know what to do with myself, especially when it came to girls. And any male my age who said he did was lying through his teeth. Females were simply in a class all by themselves.

I had had sex since that "episode" with the whore when I was eight. But I wasn't promiscuous. However, at sixteen my hormones were running wild, and girls were everywhere. I had been reinvented from a juvenile delinquent at an alternative school to a basketball and track star at one of the most respected high schools in New York City. I was tall, about six foot three now, lean and muscular. Some girls would tell me that they "liked the little boy in me." Always on cue, I would flash my toothless smile. I had lost my teeth in a basketball game at the 600 school and although I was a bit self-conscious it didn't seem to matter to them.

My relationship with Janet just fizzled out naturally. She was never "my girl." I regarded her as a friend more than anything else. But I remember her as pleasant part of my life.

I dated one girl whom I thought was so beautiful. There were two things I remember about her. Sharon looked like a black American Indian. I loved the way her black ponytail reached almost to her behind. But when I went to her house her family told her—right in front of me—that I was "too dark" for her.

There was another girl whom I'll call Mary. She knew I liked her and she would ask me for money and I would give her my lunch money again and again—just to please her. Then I found out she was giving my money to some old trifling dude from the streets.

Then there was Gloria. The first time I saw her she was in the cafeteria with two of her friends. She was tall, about five foot nine, and wore her black hair pulled back in a knot. She was about three years younger than I, and a member of the booster club, so I knew I would see her at all the afternoon games.

I'd see her watching me out of the corner of her eye as I'd pass by in my team jacket, sporting a big letter *J.* I was a letterman. Billy would be with me sometimes; we played on the basketball team together, and he'd see her looking, too. I finally broke the ice and asked her to meet me after school. She said yes.

I just wanted to talk with her and get to know her. So I walked her home from school before my practice. She was the most special girl I had ever met.

I still loved to play the congas and I did every chance I got. So I'd be there at Bernice Johnson's in Queens as often as I could. I got high from the energy when my palms and fingers would caress the skins of the drums—the touch was electric. The vibration of percussion blending with the graceful moves of the dancers was a spiritual dessert. No one really taught me how to play. But living in New York City, I was exposed to many who were masters of their craft. There was an African-Latin musical revolution taking place in the 1950s and 1960s that was unduplicated anywhere else in urban America. I had a keen ear and I would listen and watch. The many hours that Bra and I spent playing over the recordings of some of the greatest salsa musicians ever were not in vain.

Then sometimes I would sing backup with a doo-wop group in the neighborhood. We didn't have a name or anything—we didn't even have our own sound. If we sang Little Anthony & The Imperial songs, we'd sound just like them. If we sang Frankie Lymon songs, we'd sound just like him. Henry was the lead singer, a real vocal chameleon. We always said we were going to enter some of the local talent shows—but we never did.

So with the rhythm rooted deeply in my soul, I would put the Puerto Ricans and Dominicans to shame when I danced salsa. It was designed for me. You see, I would take the subway into Manhattan sometimes—alone—and go to the Palladium and watch some of the best salsa dancers I'd ever seen. Then there was the rumba, an Afro-Cuban dance, that incorporated salsa and African dance. I just loved it. Soon I stopped watching and started dancing; it was magic—those trumpets blowing and congas going and those pretty little senoritas spinning—it all just penetrated my Psyche and I was swept away into another dimension.

Then there was the jazz side of me. There were these girls, Janice, Barbara and Lois, who lived in the projects and were playing jazz when people our age were not into it. I always considered them avant-garde and they made me pay attention to jazz. When I'd play at Bernice Johnson's, the jazz dancers would dance to the recordings of the saxophone of John Coltrane, the keyboards of Thelonius Monk and the mute trumpet of Miles Davis. It was so unpretentious and unpredictable—it was so different.

So, sometimes I'd go down to the Village—always alone. I didn't have enough money to get into the clubs, so I'd stand outside. My favorite was The Village Gate. I'd stand outside for hours just to experience the mastery of the musicians playing inside. I'd close my eyes to block out any distractions. Oddly, no one bothered me. But it was Greenwich Village in the 1960s. It was alive, artistic and lovingly affectionate to all who were different, nonconformist and talented.

Maybe that's why I gravitated there so much. People in The Village celebrated their differences—everyone seemed to have their own style. You could feel their confidence and security in their freedom to express themselves. Yes, there were the Beatniks, the Bohemians, and there were the creative geniuses: the writers, the painters, the intellectuals, the musicians. It was a mecca for uninhibited thought: no chain on the brain. When I was forced by my wardrobe to be different from the other kids in elementary school it hurt and angered me. But now I wanted to be different. I didn't want to be like those troubled people in my life.

Meanwhile, I was smashing all the track competition in the face. However, I was not satisfied with my long-jump performances. I questioned my ability. Was the twenty-four foot, one inch jump at the Junior Olympics a fluke? I wasn't jumping anywhere near that now.

I expected at this point to have jumped twenty-five to twenty-six feet. My discontent forced me to reach deeper inside myself. I had to search for a better way. I wanted to be the best.

Whether it was a track meet or a basketball game, if it was during the day Gloria would be there with the booster club. She'd be out there cheering for the team, especially for me, right up front where I could see her. I'd given her my team jacket to wear. I was glad to have someone there. Daddy never came, and definitely not Bert or Ma.

So everyone at Jamaica High knew she was my girlfriend. The only problem was that Gloria was young. Her parents were separated. She lived with her mother and younger brother and was not allowed to go out at night. But we would sneak around during the day. Ma wasn't home during the day, so we'd be together there.

There was another girl, Melvina, who was from Honduras. She lived in St. Albans but was around my neighborhood quite often, she was going with Johnny Roberts, who lived in the projects and that's when I met her. When she broke up with Johnny, I started seeing her.

She was about five foot five. She wore her black shoulder-length hair full and fluffy. Her mother and Ma were acquainted. Melvina would show up at some of my games, but mostly the evening ones. She was a student at Andrew Jackson High School, which meant that there was little chance that she and Gloria would run into each other. But there was no confusion, everyone at Jamaica High knew that Gloria was my girlfriend. Melvina did, too.

Gloria, I loved.

Melvina, I liked.

Everything seemed to be going right for me. The night Jamaica High played Franklin K. Lane High School, something took over inside of me. It was the beginning of the third quarter and the score was tied. Billy passed the ball to me and I did a fast break down the middle, jumped over the center and the defense and slam-dunked the ball in their faces. The crowd went wild. Life was great even though no one was there from my family to watch it, not even Gloria this time.

I was named All-American in track and field and All-City honorable mention in basketball. In 1964 I was ranked tenth among all the high school long jumpers in the United States.

Things were going along pretty well when Coach Ellis said he wanted us to attend an assembly in the gym: Some Olympians from the 1964 Olympics were going to be there to talk to us. When the time came, I was sitting in the center of the second row, I wanted to make sure I had a good seat. Mr. Schuker stood in the center of the floor with a microphone in his hand. After a few announcements and a brief introduction (which seemed forever), long-jump champion Ralph Boston, champion swimmer Donna DeVarona and champion sprinter Wilma Rudloph entered the gym.

I was in a trance as they seemed to glide across the floor in slow motion. They made such an impact with their perfectly toned bodies, wearing those standout red, white and blue Olympic warm up suits. USA in giant letters was sewn on the back of their jackets.

I listened intently as each one shared stories of personal triumph over debilitating circumstances. It was almost as if they were talking to me, only me.

Wilma Rudolph spoke of her battle with polio when she was young and how she could not walk without a brace. Nine years later she had become a Tennessee State University "Tigerbelle" and an Olympian with two gold medals and a bronze. Donna DeVaróna spoke of how girls were shut out of sports and how she competed in the 1960 Olympics at thirteen and 1964 at seventeen. She won two gold medals. Ralph Boston had a gold and a silver medal. He spoke of growing up poor in the South and coming from a family of ten children, and how he broke Jesse Owens's world and Olympic records. He too had gone to Tennessee State University.

I knew from the moment I saw and heard these great Olympic athletes, I wanted to be one of them. From that moment on I started to prepare myself for the 1968 Olympics.

I was focused and I was happy until, out of nowhere, I was presented with this situation: Melvina's mother asked Ma to take Melvina in because there were some problems at her home. Yes, that's right, Melvina was suddenly living in my house. I could not believe it. What was going on here?

I tried to continue on like everything was normal. Coach Ellis spoke with me regarding my plans for college. He had received many, many letters of inquiry from colleges and universities. Hearing this confirmed for me that I would never have to live in the projects again; never have to wear hand-me-down clothes again; never have to be around smack-shooting, trash-talking, felonious losers whose favorite pastime was to hang out at Mrs. Moore's Candy Store huddled around an outdated jukebox after "a hard night" on the streets.

I was going to college. I was going to be an Olympian. I was going to marry Gloria.

I ran. I ran in the heat. I ran in the rain. I ran in the snow. It did not matter what the weather was. I ran when I was hurt; I ran when I was exhausted; I ran when I didn't feel well.

I ran for a dream that I was going to be someone special.

In 1965 I was ranked second in the long jump in the United States with a best of twenty-five feet three and one-half inches. I did not know a thing about the business side of the sport I was in. Nor did I know a thing about what to do with recruiters. I didn't know what questions to ask anyone. And even though my grades limited the list of schools that I could attend, I still was over my head. USC wanted me and I really wanted to go to St. John's. I declined their offers because I did not feel I could compete academically. I did not want to set myself up for failure. No one other than myself was involved in this process. Daddy certainly had no interest in being involved.

Unfortunately, I had heard wild stories about recruiters offering sports cars, clothes, apartments and such, and to a poor boy from Queens that stuff sounded pretty exciting. So naive and silly me would get on the phone with these guys and asked them flat out if they were going to give me a sports car, a wardrobe and spending money. They would damn near hang up in my face.

Dr. Leroy Walker, the track coach from North Carolina College, called to say that he would like to come to New York and talk with me and my family. Several members of his track program had become Olympians. Of course I didn't turn him down; still it seemed so odd that he would fly in just to see me.

When he got to my place, I was home alone. He was a trim, elegant man with a deep, commanding voice. I could tell he was very, very educated. He sat down and told me that he wanted me to come to his school. He said that he would personally see to it that I'd receive a college education. I was fidgeting, probably sensing that I was over my head. But I had a job to do, so I asked my usual questions about the car, wardrobe and spending money. Dr. Walker smiled and told me that what he had to offer me was an education and athletics. Period. Then he stood up and told me to think about his offer, he had to leave because he had a plane to catch.

His offer went in one ear and out the other.

Coach Ellis wanted me to consider going to Texas Southern University in Houston. His suggestion, too, went in one ear and out the other. I figured if other athletes were receiving perks, then I wanted them. So I continued with my pursuit for the right deal.

Melvina continued her persistent pursuit of me. Living under the same roof invited regular cohabitation, and I never said no, and she began pressuring me to break up with Gloria.

"I *love* Gloria," I would tell her over and over.

I wasn't smart enough to resist the constant temptation and convenience of a live-in sex mate. I was eighteen and a senior in high school and my hormones were raging. I was not mature for my age at all. In fact, I probably had the mentality of a fifteen-year-old in some areas.

I never thought of myself, as "a good catch." I didn't know how other people saw my accomplishments. I had no idea what to expect from success, other than the superficial material trappings that are most often associated with it, nor how to use the concept in preparation for an athletic competition or in preparation for life. It was like I was tripping out on a dream that I had created from watching half-hour television shows. I was no longer nervous that the dream would end. Trouble would go away—tune in next week—or at least it wouldn't hurt much. All my energies had been expended on surviving, not thriving; on staying alive, not living. "Making it" meant a big house, a new car, a new wardrobe and spending money. I definitely wanted to go to college. But I wanted to go to college mostly to train for the Olympics and to excel in sports. The education part was not real yet.

I was stumbling trying to make a decision about what college to attend. Ma and family were not interested in my athletic or educational pursuits at all; I couldn't even talk to them about it.

One afternoon, we were all over at Daddy's place. He was drunk as a skunk.

"You better help Bobby with some of them papers that he's doing," Ma said. "Shoot, a man flew in all the way from North Carolina just to talk to him. He left some stuff at my place."

"So what? I am supposed to stop what I'm doing just 'cause you say so, huh? Besides North Carolina ain't that far away."

"Well, he's your son."

Daddy stopped dead cold. His eyes were bloodshot. He could hardly sit up straight in the chair. He stared Ma down. I thought he was going to hit her.

"You goddamn liar," he yelled.

Then he looked at me and said, "I'm not your goddamn Daddy. I was in Sing-Sing when your mama made you."

You could have heard a pin drop in that room.

"You were never suppose to tell him that. He was never supposed to know. Oh, my God. Oh, my God," Ma sobbed as she clutched a pillow to her stomach and rocked uncontrollably on the sofa.

Bert and everybody started crying, including Daddy.

I just sat there. I had had no idea. All this time I thought he was my Daddy. I did not ask any questions. I stood up and walked out the door.

I don't remember anything else about that day.

* * *

Senior prom night came and went, but I was not there. I could not take Gloria; she was too young and her mother wouldn't let her go. Besides, I could not afford a tuxedo, though I'm sure that if I'd really wanted to go I would have worked something out.

My head was somewhere else. I just wanted to get the hell out of New York. I hardly had time alone so that I could think. There was no peace at Ma's, especially now. Melvina was now more aggressive about Gloria. She even threatened to "kick her ass."

I wanted to get as far away from New York as I could get— away from all the venomous people who were always waiting to poison anything that was positive. New York and poison were one and the same to me: the Big Apple was full of worms.

Then I was invited by the Amateur Athletic Union to compete in Puerto Rico and Trinidad. I was too cool when I had to go to the passport office to apply for my passport, attempting to act like this was something I had been exposed to before. Yeah, right.

It was my first airplane ride. It was my first time outside of New York. There were palm trees and ocean all around. I found the entire scene very interesting. I liked the idea of traveling.

At the AAU meets I won first place in the long jump, triple jump *and* high jump. I was a jumping machine. I had an appetite for this and I wanted more. Plus, I think being away from the pressure of that home situation may have propelled me to another level. However, as the plane touched down back home in New York, lies and deception were again waiting to smack me in the face.

I went straight home. I couldn't wait to tell somebody about my trip. I was full of stories about my first time out of New York, my first airplane ride and the medals I had won.

Soon as I hit the door, before I could put down my bag, Ma said, "Why didn't you tell me that Melvina was having your baby?"

"How you know it's my baby? I'm not the only one she's been with."

"Did you sleep with her?"

What could I say.

"Be a man and do the right thing by that girl, now."

God help me. I had just been out of New York for the first time in my life. I felt like I was suffocating. I left the house, went to a pay phone and called Gloria. I had missed her so much; I couldn't wait to see her. When I did I hugged her tight. I didn't tell her about Melvina being pregnant. It was a nightmare and I thought it would go away.

Paul Underwood was an alumnus of North Carolina Agricultural and Technical College. He wanted to recruit me to be on their track and field team. He said they would give me a full scholarship. Of course, I asked him about "the perks."

Underwood ran off a this-is-what-you'll-get litany of a car, a wardrobe, a house and spending change. This was it. *This* was my deal. Shoot, I didn't do so bad representing myself— and it couldn't have come at a better time, I thought.

It was a Saturday morning. Ma had a card game in the kitchen that had been going on all night. I rolled out of bed, washed up and greeted everyone. The room smelled of stale cigarettes and cigars and cheap whiskey.

"Bobby, Reverend Dawkins's gonna marry ya and Melvina this mornin'. Yo Daddy's gonna come here and git ya and take ya. Better git dressed," she said, still looking down at her hand of cards.

I did not answer. I did not argue. I went back to my room like an obedient robot and sat. I didn't think. I didn't move. It wasn't until Daddy came that I got dressed.

I was still in denial.

When we got to Reverend Dawkins' house, he already had a license, Melvina had already selected the music. They even had rings. Melvina's mother was there.

Melvina just stood there like a thief ready to steal my name and disrupt my dreams. It looked like both she and her mother were quite prepared for this fiasco.

I felt like I had been dropped inside a black-and-white movie: moody and mysterious like a film noir. It felt like I was in *Casablanca* or *North by Northwest*. But the star of this script was not Humphrey Bogart or Cary Grant; the star was me, Bob Beamon. There was music. Here I was—the star—but I had- n't rehearsed my lines; I was unconscious but I was walking.

I stood before Reverend Dawkins with my head bowed down.

"You don't have to do this if you don't want to," I thought I heard him say.

Why didn't I say something then? What kept me from running?

"Be a man..." I heard Ma's voice in my head. "Be a man."
I did not look up during the entire ceremony. I don't even
remember saying, "I do"—Melvina probably said it for me.

Who bought the rings? Why did Ma have Melvina living
with us? She'd never been involved with my girlfriends before.
Maybe I should have told Melvina's mother about her other
escapades. Naw, that would've broken her heart, and she had
always been nice to me.

So eager not to offend, I was. I didn't realize or even think
about what this ceremony would do to my heart and mind.

When the ceremony was over, Melvina went home and I
went to see Gloria and told her what had just happened. Of
course, she was devastated—she cried and cried. My heart
sank to the ground. I withdrew from reality. I was good at
blocking things out when I wanted to. I needed to keep myself
from being drained of my emotions, my dreams, my hopes—
and my determination.

It was like a conspiracy of narrow-minded, self-serving
people who could not stand my successes, who hovered over
me and sought to drain my energy like vampires. Evil and
trickery were disguised as concern and responsibility. I know
now that I was not alone—someone was watching over me.
Maybe the pure passion in my heart to succeed and will my
dreams into reality was stronger than the desire of others to
destroy them. It was a mental game—a battle of wills.

What would you have me do? I didn't think about asking
for a pregnancy test or talking to a doctor, nor was that information offered to me. I trusted my grandmother; after all, she
was the only person who looked out for me. Without her, I
would have been an orphan. It never occurred to question her.
Was I naive? Maybe. But it was more a matter of unconditional trust in Ma, a blind faith that made me obey her demands
even though my gut feeling persisted that this was wrong. My
body was trying to tell me something. My stomach was erupt-

ing like water boiling on a stove.

I know now the sinister effect that growing up abandoned and without affection, loving touches, kisses, and hugs has on a child. Expose that child to constant negative responses to his person, even to his presence. Make it clear to him that even seeing him is so unpleasant that his presence ignites contempt, nasty and mean words, frowns and disgust.

Add the physical abuse of beatings and kicks—again and again. What happens to the child? He is damaged by the lack of insight and experience that might enable him to process the fear and confusion, to put his relationships in perspective. What happens to the child? He will see himself as the culprit—it's his fault he is mistreated.

I was confused about Ma's love for me. I convinced myself that she knew what was best for me. She claimed me when I was a baby. She brought me home with her from Aunt Carly's. Now that I knew some of the story—that I'm sure those in the know had been whispering about for years—I felt more attached to her on the one hand and more confused about her on the other. Daddy was not my biological father, but I didn't know that then. My mother, his wife, conceived me with another man. Yes, Daddy had been in Sing-Sing for three years before it happened. But it happened. Ma made me a part of the family anyway. She kept her promise to my mother. Yes, she did. How could I not trust her with all my heart?

I loved Gloria. I loved her inner beauty, the sound of her voice and the gleam in her eyes when she looked at me. It hurt me to see her hurt. I promised her that I would get it all straightened out and divorce Melvina. But I didn't know what the hell I was doing. I was over my head, once again in foreign territory. I wanted to escape, but I couldn't. I should have seen it coming, but I didn't.

I think many of my teachers and others thought that I planned this. They probably thought that I had fallen into that inner-city pattern: a star athlete, with the whole world ahead of him, straps himself down with a baby and a wife, dragging along a whole load of baggage before he has had an opportunity to pull himself up.

I was too embarrassed to tell anyone, other than Gloria, what had happened. But of course, the new Mrs. Beamon was all over the place showing off the ring that she had bought for herself.

Dream number one, down the drain. No *Ozzie and Harriet*-like family for me. Before, at least I liked Melvina. After this, I could hardly stand to be around her.

Chapter Six

I Believed I Could Fly

Even with all the baggage that added weight to my wings, I still took flight. In January 1966, I graduated from Jamaica High as an All-American in track and field, with a scholarship from North Carolina A&T, an unbroken Junior Olympics record and a New York State record. I also had my dreams intact of making the 1968 Olympic team. I was nineteen going on twenty.

"You can run but you can't hide," Joe Lewis had said years earlier. But I didn't know that at the time. So I ran to Greensboro, North Carolina, with my pipe dreams in tow. A&T (as it's called for short) was going to be my mecca, I thought, so I reported to the athletic department, anticipating that I would walk out that day with keys to a car, keys to an apartment, the name of the store to buy the new wardrobe, an envelope full of spending cash and of course, my class and schedule materials.

I was all ready for an immediate lifestyle change. Man, did I get it. No matter that I grew up in the inner-city of New York and I was a bona fide New Yorker. You don't realize what these things mean until you are zapped out of your environment.

It was culture shock. I was in the South, where I said I would never end up. Lesson number one: never say never.

People had this slow-talking, slow-walking demeanor about them. It was green and pretty and the pace was thirty miles per hour and I was zooming at 120 miles per hour. Got the picture?

But I can't say that I was ever troubled with racism there. I guess I was isolated from it by being on a black campus. My recollection was that I did not need to leave New York City to come South to drink wine on the corner—and that's what I had gotten into.

You see, when I showed up at the athletic department, the perks that Paul Underwood promised did not exist. He lied to me and used the perks as bait to get me there. They didn't even have the right equipment or coaching staff to enable me to train. And to add insult to injury, to give me all those things—car, apartment, wardrobe and cash—the athletic director informed me, was against NCAA policy—even in its most liberal application.

I was out of there in a semester and a half. I figured it this way: Melvina had already crushed one dream. I was not about to stay in a place that could not stimulate and motivate me to seek out my other dream. I was serious about going to the Olympics and in North Carolina I found myself sliding into a dangerous rut.

More than nine months had passed since the wedding. I should have been a father by now, right? Melvina told me over the phone when I was still at A&T that she had miscarried the baby. What a liar! My deep-down unspoken suspicion had been confirmed. I knew in my heart that there had never been a baby, even though she and Ma kept telling me there had been.

I figured as long as I was away, none of it really mattered anyway. But now I had to come back to New York.

It was almost winter, 1966. I wanted to be an Olympian more than ever and I needed to get settled some place and focus.

"Boy, ya needs to forget all this here college junk. Ya needs to git out there and git some kind of job to support yo wife," Ma kept saying. However, Melvina was working and doing better than me financially, so I felt no compulsion to abandon my dreams to fulfill hers.

Coach Ellis told me that Coach Vandenberg had heard I was available and was interested in talking to me. In the college track-and-field circuit, news traveled fast. Then the call came, just like I hoped to God it would. It was Wayne Vandenberg, the track coach from University of Texas at El Paso (UTEP), formerly known as Texas Western.

Vandenberg wanted to know if it was true that I had left A&T. I told him it was. He just came right out and said if I wanted to long jump for him, he would see that I had a full scholarship to go to UTEP. I didn't hesitate. I told him yes.

I packed a couple of bags, took some of my albums, and got on a plane to El Paso. UTEP's basketball team had played the University of Kentucky in the NCAA finals, which I saw on TV. I remembered that mostly black, mostly inner-city New Yorkers comprised the team. You didn't see all-black teams that much then. So I knew about UTEP—or at least I thought I did.

Wayne Vandenberg was called "The Mouth." He was a twenty-six-year-old white guy from Chicago who had written me in my senior year asking that I consider his program when he was at the University of New Mexico. When he left New Mexico to build a track program at UTEP, he wanted to see if I was available. Perfect timing.

My first impression when I arrived at UTEP? I saw lots and lots of white people and poor Mexicans. Where are the black people? I thought maybe I should have asked more questions.

My second impression? El Paso was a border town. It was so barren and the landscape was colored in shades of taupe and gray. Giant Confederate flags flapping in the dusty wind dotted the landscape with lots of red and a little blue. During the cab ride to the campus, we passed by one pickup truck after another driven by bandanna-wearing, crusty red-faced white males with double-barreled shotguns racked to the rear window. Tumbleweed was rolling in our path and on the sides of the road, kicking up dust as it went. The twangs of Boots Randolph's music blasted from damn near every diner, truck stop or car radio as I rode toward the campus.

Mr. New York meet the desert of El Paso, Texas.

The black athletes were known as "scholarship Negroes." Other than the barely two percent black population in El Paso, UTEP's Negroes were the only American black folks north of the border. I thought I was coming to a black university. Man, that basketball team sure was deceiving. I did not realize that ninety-eight percent of the blacks at UTEP were the other male athletes.

El Paso was a thousand miles away from the "Heart of Texas." It was a suburb of Mexico. The campus was big but it was bone-dry and, oh so bare. But I tried hard not to dwell on the negative. My dormitory room was fine. I was ready to get down to business.

Coach Vandenberg tickled me as he pranced around campus like the hotshot track coach he thought he was. Pundits would always say that Vandenberg was a great recruiter—and a great recruiter does not necessarily make a great coach. But he seemed to have the respect of his athletes and he seemed to be a strong motivator.

Coach Ellis had given me a very strong fundamental base from which to build. I had always had my own style of jumping and I was no different now.

So I took the motivation from Vandenberg, the fundamentals from Ellis, and the style from me—and I developed my own training program.

I knew that my weakness was in sprinting; that's why I had started jumping—because I did jumping so much better. So each day, I would run four hours: two hours in the morning and two hours in the afternoon.

Training was different then. I did not use machines, free

weights or even magnets to revitalize the body after a training session or competition. I bounced on stretches, which we know now we shouldn't. Massage therapy, whirlpools and ultrasound were only used for the injured. I was never injured, but I would take an occasional whirlpool bath to relax.

Kenny Anderson and Roger Young were my roommates. They both stood about five foot ten and weighed between 160 and 170 pounds. Kenny was a gifted sprinter from the Bronx who had overcome a bout with spinal meningitis. He was the studious type. Roger was a triple jumper from Queens, and liked to instigate confrontations with rednecks.

Paul Gibson was white and Southern-bred from a small Texas town. He was blond, six foot three, 230 pounds of solid muscle. He was a hurdler. In the beginning, Paul set Roger off because Paul was gawking at him.

"What's your problem, white boy?" Roger demanded.

"Look, I don't mean no harm but I ain't never been around coloreds before. I mean y'all is different, but y'all ain't different. I just can't figure it out," Paul said in a low, Texas drawl.

Roger shoved a clenched fist in his face.

"Figure this out, punk," he said.

But Roger couldn't incite Paul. All in all, the team liked Paul, partly because he was pretty much down-to-earth and seemingly without any hidden agendas.

I had to declare a major as soon as I registered, so I chose physical education. I'd go to class, do some homework, train, go back to the dorm, do some homework and be bored as hell. We'd be doing all kinds of stuff—like throwing water-filled balloons out of the windows on the heads of whoever was unfortunate enough to walk out the door first. We would set some of the rooms on fire just enough to cause an evacuation and for days we attempted to spike the water cooler in the cafeteria with Spanish fly—too many watchful eyes to pull that one off.

UTEP had a student body of about 10,000. Out of that

number, 250 were black. Out of the 250 blacks, about 230 were male athletes, five were male non-athletes and fifteen were females. That adds up to fifteen black females at UTEP for 235 young black males in their prime.

We had no social outlets and interracial dating was strictly taboo. So we threw water balloons on people, drank beer and played practical jokes on one another.

Some of the team would go across the border to Juarez on the weekend to party and have sex. But not me. The school was well equipped to handle the hazards of these escapades. All a person had to do was go to the Infirmary and get treated with antibiotics for gonorrhea and other social diseases which they picked up over there—they were even prepared for syphilis. But I mainly went across the border to Juarez for one thing: to buy custom-tailored pants for ten dollars.

Everyone was talking about *In the Heat of the Night* starring Sidney Poitier and we went to the movie theater downtown to see it. Poitier played Virgil Tibbs, a black Philadelphia detective who comes down to this small Southern town of Sparta, Mississippi, to conduct a murder investigation. There he butts heads with its racist, small-town police chief played by Rod Steiger.

El Paso was not unlike Sparta. Like the time when Kenny, Roger, Paul and I stopped at a convenience store to buy a few snacks and toiletries. When we got to the counter, there were three troublemakers who kept staring at us. When Kenny put his items on the counter, including a can of deodorant spray, one of the renegades commented to his friend, "Did you know niggers used deodorant?"

Roger came out of nowhere and said, "What did you say? Huh? Repeat it. Repeat it loud enough so everybody can hear you. Don't be no coward now, you cracker motherfucker."

The store clerk was nervous, as was I. He asked everyone to please pay for their merchandise and leave the store. The troublemakers obliged but not without first assuring us that they were going outside to get their guns.

Roger was walking behind them as they reached the door, yelling, "Yeah, motherfuckers, go get your shit 'cause we gonna kick your asses."

"Shut the fuck up, Rog. You ain't speaking for me," I said.

Here these racist-crazed sons of bitches had rifles and handguns, and this stupid unarmed black fool was going to get us all killed. But we had to leave the store: we couldn't stay inside forever.

When we walked out the front, the trio had armed themselves from inside their roving arsenals. This was Texas, the fucking wild, wild west. Everybody was "packing." It was part of being a Texan. Yeah, everyone was packing except us.

They pointed their guns directly at us; we all froze. Now big-mouth Roger had nothing to say.

But Paul spoke up. He told them that we were his Negroes from UTEP; that he was a track star and since he was the only one with a car, he agreed to take us to the store.

"If anything happens to them, then I am the one in big trouble. I just can't see losing my scholarships over some dumb, stupid-ass niggers. I mean come on, they ain't worth a damn."

One of the tobacco-spitting creatures mumbled something to the other two.

"Shucks man, we thought you was some kind of nigger lover. See, we were gonna shoot your ass, too. Now get the fuck outta here and I wouldn't come back this way if I was y'all," the short one said.

Then he walked over and slugged Roger right on his jawbone and knocked him to the ground. They walked away and then sped off in their pickup, leaving a trail of desert dust behind them. Just like in a John Wayne film.

*   *   *

Back in New York, Melvina was lost in a sea of confusion.

She must've convinced herself that once she got married to me, she would cease to be an outsider in my life. She apparently was unprepared for the consequences of her deceit. I lived my life as though she did not exist. I rarely called her. I never thought of her with affection. My secret desire to have a real family had been shattered by her and my grandmother's intrusion into my dreams of marital bliss. I battled with myself to keep this character from distracting me. She wasn't going to swipe this dream away, too.

* * *

By now I had changed my major from physical education to speech and drama. Mrs. Mary Manchuca was my favorite professor in my major. I admired her zeal and passion for teaching. She kept me excited about learning.

I felt the same way about Mrs. Alice Kiska, my English professor. Mrs. Manchuca and Mrs. Kiska told me that if I was going to be in the public eye I had to be prepared to express myself. I had to be able to do this with confidence and professionalism. They decided to coach me in English grammar, speaking and public presentation. I approached my academic workouts with the same intensity as I approached my athletic ones.

I remember the first time I had to make a speech in class. I forgot what I wrote but I do remember having a nervous stomach for days in anticipation of this milestone I was approaching. When it was my turn, I took a gym bag and walked outside the classroom door. Then moments later, I came back in bouncing a basketball and wearing gym shorts. I walked over to the microphone and said, "Thank God, I'm physically fit."

I was nervous, but the class apparently liked the way I started off because they applauded. Man, it was easy from there. The rest of my speech on "Staying Physically Fit" came out so smoothly. I felt so comfortable up there, nothing like I

thought I'd feel. When it was over everyone applauded. I was
very happy. That day marked the end of my fear of speaking in
public.

Then I performed "cold readings." In one of my classes, I
performed a scene from "Lilies of the Field," that included a
song, "Shenandoah." My class was shocked when I ended the
scene by singing the song.

"Beamon, you can really sing," said a classmate. "We
were all shocked, we couldn't believe that voice was coming
from you. Right on!"

* * *

Eventually, Melvina moved to El Paso. She bought a
house, got a job and set up housekeeping. I have to admit, living in the house was much more comfortable than living in the
dorm.

When I lived in the dorm, the guys had a calendar on the
wall in our room, where we'd check off the days until we could
go back to New York. Kenny couldn't take it any longer. He
left UTEP and went to Ohio State.

George McCarty was UTEP's athletic director,
Vandenberg's boss. He was short and bald and smoked a cigar.
There was one memorable thing about McCarty; he called all
his scholarship Negroes, "niggers" or "nigras."

He told Jack Olsen, a writer with *Sport Illustrated*, that he
was doing the best he could. He was born and bred in the South
and he grew up calling Negroes, niggers. This is the man who
was in charge of ninety-five percent of the black students at
UTEP.

This, then, was what was happening in the world of college
sports: Major white universities were recruiting black athletes
to gain recognition and titles in their college sports programs.
Before this, many extraordinary black athletes had no choice
but to play for black colleges and universities. But now these

big white universities took notice of the reservoir of black talent. Things were changing. A school with a winning team brings more revenue into the school. So now the Negro athlete was in high demand.

What became real to the black athletes when they arrived at the white school was that academics were the last thing on the school's list for them to accomplish. House them, feed them, stroke their ego and give them a little scholarship. Again, someone was watching over me. I flourished personally and academically under the tutelage of Mrs. Manchuca and Mrs. Kiska. I was training my mind and my body.

Every morning, just after sunrise, I was out on those barren foothills. Time was short to prepare for the 1968 Olympics. Time seemed to be passing so slowly, yet like a train rounding a bend, it would begin to pick up speed as it approached its intended destination.

I found myself at a long-jump competition, alongside my hero, Ralph Boston, and a Los Angeles high school kid, Jerry Procter. In a flash, Procter had outjumped both me and Ralph. This was a wakeup call for me.

"How could a high school kid beat me?" I lamented over and over.

I didn't even deal with the fact that he had beat Ralph Boston, too. I was concerned about my performance. I promised myself that I would never be beaten again because of over confidence. I searched my soul and had to admit to myself that I had not taken Procter seriously.

From then on, when I entered a competition, I would concentrate on visualizing my own performance. I would say a prayer before every jump. I would not be concerned about, or listen to, what the other person might or might not do or say.

Then came the NCAA finals. I was favored in the triple jump and the long jump. Calvin Hill was the one to beat in the triple jump (his son, Grant Hill, is now a major talent in the NBA.). I did not focus on Calvin, though. Instead, I remained quiet and went off by myself before the jump. I closed my eyes and "saw" myself running down the runway, leaping off the boards and jumping, one-two-three, into the sandpit.

When my name was called, I focused inwardly and my body seemed to be on "automatic", as if in a playback of my previous mental performance. When it came time for the long jump, I would follow the same cadence in my mind: relax, focus, pray and "see."

When the sand settled, I had literally flown over the pit. My work on the sprint had paid off and I had perfected the rhythm of the speed I needed to maximize the takeoff from the runway. I used my upper body and arms in synchronization with the vibrations of the drums playing in my head. What appeared on the outside was an aerodynamically designed human takeoff and landing.

The next day, the headline on a sports page read, BOB BEAMON: NCAA TRIPLE AND LONG JUMP CHAMPION. But this was not the time to relax; this was the time to work harder. I could smell the aroma of the Olympics; I could taste the flavor of winning. I dreamed about trading Olympic pins, collecting all the sponsor giveaways and sporting those official Olympic warm-ups. Being courted by shoe companies and apparel manufacturers for television commercials, corporate endorsements, public relations opportunities—these were dreams that I had not dared to dream, yet.

* * *

Even champions like Wilt Chamberlain, who was MVP for the Philadelphia 76ers, were not sought out for the kind of endorsement opportunities available to decathlon champion Bob Mathias, or to Don Drysdale, Pete Rose or Johnny Unitas. But I would not entertain any thoughts too long that would taint my dreams of a better life.

We were the Miners, the UTEP Miners, and the track athletes were the stars. We stood out so vividly in this environment of taupe and gray. We were dark brown, light brown, medium brown, blue-black—our hues spanned shades of sepia, beige, cinnamon, mahogany, pecan, ebony, sienna, yellow and red. Our bodies were sculpted like the Greek statutes of the athletes in the ancient Olympic Games in Ancient Greece. Our gracefulness was reminiscent of ballet dancers as we stretched, sprinted and projected our bodies through the air like birds.

But, as a group, we were so unhappy there. And it was all about race: not the foot race but the human race.

Jack Olsen, who was writing a series on the black athlete for *Sports Illustrated*, wrote that I was naive because I asked questions like, "Can you explain something to me: How can people hate one another?" and, "Why is it that white people are so prejudiced against colored people?"

Was it naive to question the venom that poisoned people's hearts and minds? I don't think so. I wanted to know why I had to cross a picket line in New York City, my damn hometown, in order to compete in a track meet. You know why? The meet was being held at New York Athletic Club and they didn't admit blacks, but each year profited big time from their sponsored meets that consisted of mostly black athletes.

Most of us were just too homesick to pass up a trip to New York. We had been counting the days. I was dying to see Gloria. I was quoted in the same article as saying, "We hadn't been home for a long time, and we were miserable in El Paso, and here was a chance to visit our people with all expenses paid."

Our decision to cross the picket line certainly made Vandenberg happy. He was counting on us to bring in a championship and we were desperate to get out of El Paso. But we would learn that that decision was nothing compared to the one we had to make next. Our next meet was between Utah State and Brigham Young University. Someone on our team called our attention to the fact that BYU was a Mormon school. The

Book of Mormon castigates the black race as inferior and descended from the devil. We went ballistic.

Nine of us from the team including Dave Morgan, a quarter-miler, and Kelly Myrick, a hurdler, went to Vandenberg and told him we were not going to compete in Utah.

After a couple of days of meetings, emotions flaring, Vandenberg and Assistant Athletic Director Bowden talked to us for the last time about our positions and the consequences of our actions. It was simple: Boycott the meet in Utah and your scholarship would be history. It was a major deal. News organizations from all over the world, including *The New York Times*, reported this incident.

Thus, I lost my scholarship but, damn it, I wasn't going to lose my dream. I continued training for Mexico City. Being an Olympian was not going to be a dream deferred.

Not for me.

Chapter Seven

Think!

The hollow isolation of El Paso had proven to be the perfect location for my training regimen for the Olympics. Every Friday I would challenge the most extreme obstacle courses. Starting the weekend, still on the edge, going deeper inside myself, I relentlessly focused on pushing my athletic talents to their maximum performance.

I imagined how it must have looked: my image blurred against the orange-red-gold backdrop of the rising sun, my long, slender silhouette sprinting up forty-seven stories of stone mountain, to the cadence of a drumbeat. *Boom...boom...boom* was the rhythm that played in my head "sho-bo-tee-bop-arittle-rittle-barn," I scatted over and over like a Gregorian monk's chant, until my inner music became automatic. In the beginning, shinsplints pained my movements as the impact of the stone surface against the bones, muscles and tendons of my feet, legs and knees flirted with the probability of permanent injuries. My persistence in this form of training would not permit the outside voices of doubt to penetrate my inside power of focus. Building the level of endurance mattered. Making the Olympic team, visiting Mexico City, winning an Olympic gold medal and being able to finish college and land a decent job—that's what mattered.

Being alone on the mountain with only me to listen to sometimes took me back to the snarls and callousness I lived with in my youth: I'd feel again the sunken sensation in my gut from too little nourishment; see again the goose bumps as I shivered violently during the long chilling nights without heat. The isolation on that mountain brought back the fear that I never did and never would belong to anyone. It recalled my reluctance to speak up, to withdraw, not to make waves and chance being left alone, again. Hindsight is always twenty-twenty, and I would only allow the intrusion into my concentration to be the briefest of brief. As I dissolved deeper and deeper into my training, those thoughts would be the farthest from my mind. This was not the time to be distracted by anything or anyone.

Melvina thought that when she moved to Texas I would be forced to acknowledge her and accept her as my wife. What Melvina could not grasp was that a legal ceremony forced upon me could not force me to love her. Even though we lived in the same house, I did not include her in my school or sports activities. I still felt betrayed, disappointed and confused. How could my grandmother be a party to this? I could not understand it. But, it mattered little to me. I was on a mission. I had a chance to make a difference in my life, and I wasn't going to let anyone or anything get in my way, especially not my farce of a marriage.

* * *

Damn near everything that happened in 1968 was important and had far-reaching results. It was a time for the emotions of a society to erupt over the ills and the greed that had been pent up under the fabric of democracy. What did the words *rights* and *freedom* really mean? I had learned from an early age that I would be stupid to think that the definitions of *those* words included people like me. How could that be possible? I asked myself more than once. Then someone explained to me that at one time blacks were considered property and not people, that we were not included in the intentions of the drafters of the laws of the land, therefore, the laws did not include people like me. Only white people. But doesn't it say *people?*

Every place I went in the United States was the scene of some ridiculous confrontation that had to do with race. I'd been sheltered by the cloak of poverty from the in-your-face racism of the white world, so therefore I figured that on the other side of poverty was an intelligent, compassionate world, free of bullshit. Was I wrong. Bullshit, I quickly learned, is everywhere, from the New York Athletic Club that would not admit blacks and Jews, to Brigham Young University that compared black people to demons (except when they wanted to use them to win their basketball and football games and run their track-and-field competitions.). In Texas, they wanted to cut off our heads and hang them as trophies in their run-down, dusty bars.

But I was used to being alone, whether I was surrounded by a crowd of people in the city or a pile of tumbleweed in the middle of a desert. So I blocked out the arrogance of ignorant people so blind and tainted. I could not allow them to penetrate my mind or my heart or my body. So I focused so intensely that I shut out everything. Nothing, absolutely nothing, was going to distract me from being in the best shape, from having the strongest legs, from having the fastest speed coming down the long-jump runway, from enduring the longest challenge. Nothing.

So I blocked out the nagging discomfort that Melvina brought to my life. I blocked out the constant name-calling of "nigger this" and "nigger that" coming from mouths of children, bums, lawmakers, law enforcers, rich, poor and UTEP's George McCarthy, the athletics director who apologized that his "upbringing made it hard to call them anything else." I blocked out the political war that raged all around me. It was a personal war as well. How could I help anyone else if I couldn't help myself?

This was my chance to escape the hellfires of Jamaica,

Queens, the envious venom coming from all those I knew, especially all those I knew as family. This was my chance to escape
the glares and eyeball rolling, the reminders that "you still ain't
no better than us," and all the ones who became nice to me
when they thought I was rich and could give them things.
Come to think of it, I thought I was rich, and I was, compared
to what I had as a child.

The quantum force that drove inside me was more potent
than ever before. I wanted this. I really wanted this. Oh, how
I wanted this! All the energy that I could muster ran through
my legs and my arms. All the pain of being knocked and
stomped as a kid, the hollowness of being left alone, abandoned, the fear of being invisible forever, the rage that brewed
inside me that I wouldn't dare release its velocity would flatten
a city block—all this pulsated inside me and it became my high
octane fuel. I now know there's a word for what I did with all
those feelings. It's called sublimation. Thank God, there's such
a thing as sublimation. Had I channeled those powerful energies in an antisocial way, I could have been a criminal monster,
a one-man crime wave, a brutal murderer, an armed robber, you
name it. But there was something stronger than the rage and the
anguish that grew inside me...something.

I knew I could fly. During my workouts, during the day,
during the night, I would constantly visualize the jump in my
head. I saw every detail: my legs extending straight ahead of
me, my heart pounding to the rhythm of the congas, my arms
and upper body meeting my knees in midair. Each new day
began with the same routine. I was no-nonsense and serious.
This meant the world to me. It was my turn.

* * *

Lake Tahoe tugged at my soul. I could not wait to get there
for the Olympic trials and get that part over with so I could start
preparation for Mexico City. Then, on June 5, 1968, it hap-

pened. Unbelievably, it happened. Bobby Kennedy was assassinated at the Ambassador Hotel in Los Angeles. You know, he was going to be our next president. There was a poison being consumed in our land. I felt so sad to see America like this. *Damn! Now Bobby's gone,* I thought, only two months after the assassination of Dr. Martin Luther King, Jr., which was shocking enough, not to mention what the murder of President Kennedy did to me. I was seventeen when President Kennedy was killed, and I felt like I wanted to take the boys from the projects down to Dallas and kick some ass. I felt helpless and stunned. But Bobby Kennedy and Martin Luther King, Jr., were almost back to back. Not more riots and fires, I sighed. *What the hell is going on with The United States of America?* I hoped it would still be around for me to see what freedom would be like and if my dreams could happen for me like Dr. King preached—and like I fought so hard in my heart to believe. But this cruelty, these acts of violence; while I allowed them to distract my focus only for a nanosecond, they still hurt my heart.

The loss of these two men of substance seemed no coincidence, and their loss somehow compelled an urgency in my soul: life was too short and too precious to mess around with. Something in my heart and my body was telling me about this life adventure that I was on. Adrenaline gushed through my veins. I could not put my finger on it, but I felt I was on some kind of fascinating journey, and that each episode provided a clue of some kind to solve something, like putting together one of those giant jigsaw puzzles. Only this one was named, "The Bob Beamon Life Puzzle." I didn't know exactly where I was going in life, but I knew I was going to the Olympic Games—nothing was going to stop me from getting there.

The Olympic Trials were postponed until after Bobby Kennedy's funeral and at last the moment had arrived. When I flew into Lake Tahoe the night before the Olympic Trials, the walk through the small terminal was sort of my runway. I wanted to feel my best and look my best, so I had decided to wear a cream-colored, double-breasted suit with matching shirt, a wide, hand-painted silk necktie and brown, side-buckled shoes that I had bought the last time I was in Frankfurt, Germany, for a track meet, my first time in Europe. I had a habit of looking down at my feet when people looked at me. I still do that. Stylish clothes just lift my spirit. I like how they feel and the attention that they bring, especially from women. One very attractive, well-dressed woman in her thirties asked me where I got my shoes.

"In Europe," I answered.

"I thought so. You just don't see those here," she said with a smile as we walked in the same direction.

I started to ask her if I could buy her a drink or something, but I didn't. I could not afford any distractions, no matter how tempting.

The high altitude and dry heat of Lake Tahoe was no stranger to me, it was very similar to El Paso. As I stood in the pit waiting for the long-jump event to begin, I could feel the bubbling sensation brewing in my gut. I had had the opportunity to train with the best while there, especially champion sprinters Tommie Smith and John Carlos in the 200 meters, and NCAA 400-meter speedster champion Lee Evans, all from San Jose State. Training with other champions challenged me to reach for a higher level of performance. I was just so excited and honored to be in the company of athletes of their caliber. Then, my time came. To keep me limber, I stretched and moved as I watched the great Ralph Boston soar through the air, hang there and land in the sand. Ralph Boston was *the* man, a walking, talking bona fide legend. At the 1960 Olympics in Rome, Ralph broke Jesse Owens's record. Last year he injured his knee. But there he was, standing in the same pit as me, ready to go for his third Olympics. "Bob Beamon"—I heard my name announced. *It's time. It's time,* I said to myself I stood at the top of the runway, took a deep breath and took off.

My jump measured twenty-seven feet six and one-half inches—enough to qualify for the United States Olympic Team. Yeah, Bob Beamon was going to Mexico City. It felt oh so unreal. Other athletes came over and patted me on the back as I walked to the locker room. Pinch me? Heck, kick me! Yes, I had dreamed it. I had believed it. But, man, when it actually happened, my heart pumped, my stomach swelled, and I understood that the images that played in my mind were sacred. Prophetic? Words like this were not a part of my vocabulary.

I felt showered with pride. Here I was, standing tall next to Ralph Boston, the legend; Lee Evans, who would win the gold in the 400 meters and whose record would last for twenty years; Bill Toomey, who would win the gold in the decathlon; Tommie Smith, who would win the gold in the 200 meters; Al Oerter, the three-time Olympic gold medal discus thrower who, at age thirty-two, would win a fourth one; Dick Fosbury, who would break the high-jump record and create the backward jump that high jumpers would use from then on, called The Fosbury Flop; Wyomia Tyus, a sprinter in the hundred meters, who won two gold medals and a silver in 1964 and would win another gold in Mexico; Debbie Meyers, who would be the first swimmer to win three individual gold medals in a single Olympics and set Olympic records in the 200-, 400- and 800-meter freestyle races. Those are a few of the incredible athletes with whom I had the privilege of being teammates. The media would call us "the greatest track-and-field team of all times," and the names kept coming: Jimmy Hines, Ron Freeman, Willie Davenport, Larry James, Mel Pender, Vince Matthews, Wylie White, Martha Watson and Eleanor Montgomery. I could go on and on. "Belong" covered me and fit me like the dark fits the night and the light fits the day. I was now an *Olympian*. I had earned the right, and I claimed the title.

The next step was several weeks of training in High Altitude School in Colorado Springs, Colorado.

Things were very different in 1968. If you were paid to run

or jump or compete in any sport, you were considered to have professional status and could not compete in the Olympic Games. If you had never been paid to compete, you had amateur status and could compete in the Olympic Games. Quite different from today, when we have Dream Teams of professional athletes competing in the Olympics. But this was the time for the unbelievable to be believed anyway. It was complicated, complex and confused. The struggles between the amateur athlete (who was not allowed to be paid for their work) and promoters (who wouldn't work *unless* they were paid), were never-ending. But on the flip side, if you were a world-class competitor, you had to be in a position to train daily and compete frequently. There was no professional track and field in 1968. There were no shoe deals except when you would go to your locker and find a wad of cash stuffed in your new pair of track shoes. It was a promoter's game. They lived well and they would barter with you, buy you a car or clothes and pay your expenses and provide first-class travel to their meets. They would treat you like royalty, but you would have nary a dime in your pocket.

The Olympic movement had its dirty laundry to clean, but International Olympic Committee chief, Avery Brundage, was determined that it would not be cleaned in public. Harry Edwards, then a twenty-five-year-old, Ph.D. professor at San Jose State, was well-resented by the powers that be for his outspokenness against double standards and the oppression suffered by black athletes in America. When he announced the boycott of the Olympic Games by black athletes, Brundage quickly issued a statement to the international media whipped with venom, "I hope they [black athletes] wouldn't be foolish enough to protest at the Games because if they did, they would be sent home immediately."

I knew the deal, I did not have blinders on. White and black relations had hit an all-time low. As long as we blacks had seemingly "stayed in our place," been seen but not heard, we could pretend that we were coexisting—in our own separate little worlds. Whispering men and women with superiority complexes were blaming the G.I. Bill for using their tax money to finance our delusions of grandeur. When I heard these words coming from people's mouths, whether on the news or on the street, I would get this queasy feeling in my gut and wonder who or what gave these people the notion that they were better than anyone else just because their skin was white. They did not look smarter than me, certainly did not act any smarter than me, were not anymore attractive than me—so what was it? All I knew was that I just wanted to be treated like a human being; all I knew was that I wanted to be able "to be" without restrictions from the outside. Hell, I had my own inside battles to fight.

Kareem Abdul-Jabbar opted not to compete in Mexico City. But he was getting ready to sign a multimillion-dollar deal to play professional basketball anyway. Bill Russell, the star center for the Boston Celtics, was an outspoken supporter of the boycott. There was no question that things needed to change, and I desperately wanted things to change. But why would I want to give up my only opportunity to change my life for the better? I was not into it. I just did not feel that the boycott had been carefully planned. Anyhow, the athletes were split, and the boycott was officially called off. But the feelings were still there, just as immediate and just as strong.

I wanted to stay focused, like a laser beam. I had allowed myself a little celebration after I made the team by venturing over to the casino in Lake Tahoe. I only had about fifty dollars in my pocket, and that had to last at least four weeks. But I felt lucky, really lucky. So I gripped the sides of the roulette table and bought twenty dollars worth of chips.

"Put it all on eleven black," I instructed the dealer like I knew what I was doing.

And wouldn't you know it, "Eleven black! The gentleman in the white suit wins," he announced.

Well, if there were an award for sucker of the night, I would take first place. Instead of cashing in my one hundred dollars worth of chips and taking my butt back to my room, what did I do? You got it, I predicted the future again. Oh, I was on a roll. "Seven red?" Yes! And for ten minutes, I was king of the night. In twelve minutes, I had taken twenty dollars and parlayed it into one thousand dollars! Should I walk? Seemed like my feet were trying to move me on their own. But this was a once-in-a-lifetime feeling. This was my lucky day. I rationalized I could pay my rent and my car notes for six months and concentrate on my schoolwork. Go to Leighton Brothers in Manhattan and get a couple of suits made, take Gloria on a shopping spree at the Olympics. Oh yeah! Before I could think, my mouth said, "One thousand on eleven black!" That wheel rolled around and the dice bounced over the seven black and landed right next to it in the eight slot. In less than fourteen minutes, I had won and lost one grand! Poof, just like that. I took my broke butt to bed.

* * *

The scene during the days before the Summer Olympics in Mexico City was saturated with sportswriters and news journalists' predictions of superhuman track-and-field performances. The newspapers and television were filled with these reports. Physiologists had debated for years about the effect the rare air at 7,347 feet would have on the athletes. All I wanted to do was break the twenty-eight-foot barrier in the long jump. There were mountains of articles and news reports claiming that a number of nations wanted to have The Games moved from Mexico City because of the fear that some athletes would gain unfair advantage from the high elevations. But sports experts disagreed and stated that any performance would be relative and whoever won, won—despite the elevation. So the Games began.

After the trials, I had still been training and still been focused, even more so than before. Maybe it was a combination of having that thousand dollars slip through my hands, Melvina telling me she was coming to Mexico City, and the excitement of seeing Gloria and having her there by my side at the most incredible time of my life. Even with all the competitions I had been in since I was seventeen, I never had a loved one or family member in the stands rooting for me. Just from that personal point of view, I knew that this was even more special than I had ever imagined.

* * *

It was October 12, 1968. I arrived in Mexico City with the United States Olympic Team from Colorado Springs by way of Lake Tahoe, carrying a suitcase packed with two suits, four pairs of slacks, six shirts, three pairs of dress shoes and one pair of Puma and one pair of Adidas track shoes. A shuttle bus for the athletes took me directly to the Olympic Village to check in and be processed, as it was called. Mel Kahn, who owned Pacific Coast Track Club, had a car waiting to take me to his private villa, where I stayed during my time in Mexico. I was the number one long-jump contender, having won twenty-two of the last twenty-three competitions, and the NCAA long jump and triple jump champion. The car and the invitation to be a guest with him and his family at their villa were perks that Mel offered to me as a champion, in hopes that I would represent his track club after I won the gold medal. I was not the only athlete who was being schmoozed by a promoter.

The villa was a beautiful Mexican-style home with terra cotta floors and ceramic inlays. It was furnished in shades of orange, rust, gold and blue. Each room opened to a lovely landscaped courtyard graced with marigolds, palm trees and other plants whose names I did not know. Mel directed me to a private suite, secluded by trees and a long corridor from the rest of

the house, and told me that this was my space. It was wonderful, with three spinning ceiling fans, matching bedspread,
drapes and a sofa in those beautiful rustic colors. Yeah, I
thought, I could get used to this!

Then, I saw the graphic newspaper photographs of some of
the hundreds of University of Mexico students who had been
murdered by the police only days before. There had been mention of this in the news before I left Colorado Springs but it had
been upstaged by the coming Olympic Games. Mexican police
and soldiers, under orders from their president, brought swift,
bloody silence to their airing of internal problems: the priority
was not to be embarrassed in front of the international community. They killed two hundred and sixty students and injured
twelve hundred and six. I really felt terrible, but I could not get
caught up in it. If I had thought about it more deeply, I would
have been afraid for all the people around me and myself, so I
had to dismiss it. Protests were going on all over the world,
though this one was close, real close.

I had to keep focused no matter what. That's all I knew to
do at this point. Was this a dream that I would suddenly awak-
en from and find myself back in the trenches of South Jamaica?
Get out of my head, my inner voice demanded. Nevertheless,
those day-mares would creep into my crystal daydreams of triumph. At that point, I would immediately shake them off and
keep training and thinking. Many times I would walk off by
myself and see that jump in my mind's eye.

A few days later, Gloria arrived. Her smile and sweet scent
lit up my senses. My heart was flushed with emotion as I
hugged her tightly. She was the final touch, the icing on the
cake. This incredible feeling of connection warmed me. Hard
to put in words. For there were no words to explain this. I felt
connected to my surroundings, with Mexico City, with the
ground, with my team and with my love. I'd never belonged
like that before. Man, was it powerful!

Even when someone told me that Melvina had been at the

Olympic Village looking for me, it did not shake my faith. The nanosecond of static that I felt at the mention of her name disappeared into oblivion. I never even entertained the possibility of a confrontation with her.

The group that called for the boycott, Olympic Project for Human Rights, was well represented in Mexico City: Dr. Harry Edwards and Olympic sprinters Tommie Smith and John Carlos. There was a significant buzz among black athletes about all the racial injustices that we had been subjected to in the United States, the same country that we represented and for which we wore the red, white and blue—just like the black warriors in the Viet Nam War did. They were the ones who were maimed and killed during their mission to protect democracy. But if they survived the war, they'd come home to white ignorant yelps of "Niggers!" "That apartment's been rented" or "That job has been filled."

John Carlos and Tommie Smith apparently had not been satisfied with the low-key murmurs of discontent. There was a worldwide audience out there watching us. Destroying the dignity of a people in a so-called free land was hypocritical and unacceptable. It was wrong, and it was horrible, no matter who the perpetrators. As Fannie Lou Hamer said, we were "sick and tired of being sick and tired."

Tommie Smith sprinted to first place in the 200 meters, with John Carlos coming in third place. Their faces glowed with the pride of their achievement, especially Tommie, one of the best sprinters I had ever seen. When they mounted the winner's stand, clad in their warm ups, their black socks were exposed. As they faced the flags and the "Star Spangled Banner" played, Tommie and John bowed their heads and raised their black-leather-gloved clenched fists toward the sky, in the gesture that we had come to know as the symbol for "Black Power."

Boos from the crowd blocked out the music of the national anthem. The world was shocked and intolerant of their choice of venue to air their grievances. "It was a cry for help, not a hate message," Tommie would later say.

Brundage was beside himself with fury. He did not miss a beat in making good on his promise to expel any defiant athlete from the Games. He embraced the opportunity to make an example of Tommie and John. It was no secret that Brundage was a bigot. His disdain for blacks came out when he defied the mandates from all the other participating nations to exclude South Africa from the Games because of their inhumanity to humanity with their practice of apartheid.

The buzz surrounded me. *Jesus, what is going on here?* But I wanted to win. I told myself, *Bob, you did not come over 2,000 miles from South Jamaica not to take home a gold medal.* I was so matter of fact with myself now. Brent Musburger, a reporter, called Tommie and John "Black-skinned stormtroopers." People, angered that "they made a mockery of a sacred ceremony," cut into media coverage like a sword. A poster being forced before the camera's eye by a black demonstrator, which read "Why Be a Hero in Mexico and a Slave at Home?" could not help but haunt America.

Thank God I only stayed in the Olympic Village dormitory for a couple of days. There was so much chaos there at this point. News crews and reporters were all over the place, tripping over one another trying to get the story. Bright klieg lights stood glaring all night in the windows of athletes trying to sleep, thick black cables covered the floors of the entrances to the dorms, while reporters knocked on doors hoping for, and hanging on, any sentence that could be developed into a spot on the evening news. After they had been expelled from the Games, all Tommie and John wanted was to get out, without repeatedly answering the same questions. Brundage tried to have their medals taken away, but that did not happen. The majority of the athletes were very sympathetic to Tommie and John about what was happening to them. My villa was forty minutes away from the Village. There, it was calm; I was isolated from the insanity.

Historians ignore the fact that white high jumper Dick Fosbury raised his fist during his medal ceremony as a gesture of solidarity with Carlos and Smith's protest of human rights violations in the United States.

* * *

When I woke up the morning of October 18, the day of the long-jump event, and saw the dark clouds in the sky, I didn't know what to think. The previous night, I had made passionate love to Gloria, something that I had never done before a competition. I had committed the cardinal sin of sports, having sex before a competition. All I could think of were words that started with *D*—deplete, drain, dissipate, distract, da da da dum! *You have just left your gold medal on the sheets*, I told myself. Then I refused to think about it anymore. I thought of nothing but "the jump." I had few words for Gloria, just enough to say I'd see her at the stadium. She understood my focus and kissed me "good luck." It meant so much to me to have her there; her sweetness insisted that I remain serene.

It was terrifically humid as I stood in the stadium. The air appeared to be as thick as the clouds that loomed above my head. Just the day before, I had been so nervous and tense that I had fouled in my first two attempts in the preliminaries. If I fouled a third time I would be disqualified. I had worked so hard to maximize my speed on the runway that I had become foul prone. But Ralph came over and told me to "step back a few inches" before I made my approach.

I followed his advice and made the finals, just like Luz Long had advised Jesse Owens at the 1936 Olympics in Berlin, I later discovered. But historical facts were the farthest thing from my mind. I felt great. Ralph had helped me to overcome the obstacles. I always felt good about Ralph, always.

On that glorious day, I remember how vividly my mind

visualized the entire jump: eerily, but so very clearly. I was pumped, my adrenaline at its peak. I was motivated, I was inspired, I was relaxed. I wanted it bad! There were two jumpers before me. Each time they called a name, a surge of power would strike me like a bolt of lightning: electricity running through my veins that made me feel stronger and stronger.

I knew that I had to be as great as Ralph Boston or better. The existing world and Olympic records were jointly held by Ralph and Igor Ter-Ovanesyan of the Soviet Union. From working with him on a daily basis, I had become a much better athlete, if not from a physical standpoint, then from an emotional one. Ralph had this fierce motivation and dedication to this sport that rubbed off on me.

When they called my name, I was ready. I felt very peaceful and calm. My body was never more relaxed. There was no sound. There were no people talking, even though there were a lot of people yelling and screaming. I felt alone. I said to myself, this was going to be my day. I could not feel my legs under me, I was floating. I stood tall and straight at the head of the long runway. I shook my arms and hands to loosen up. I took the first step on the runway. After that, it was all automatic; instinct took over and lifted me from the white board, there was no sound, all I heard was the pumping of my heart. I breached barriers as if I was on a magic carpet ride. I landed with such impact that I continued to jump like a kangaroo hopping out of the sandpit. I was not happy with my landing. Hell, how could I have landed on my butt and not on my feet! *That will cost me inches*, I thought. *Damn, I messed up—I really did land on my butt—I've lost at least a foot*, I thought. I turned to see if the flag was up. There was such a tremendous roar from the spectators, I wasn't sure at first just what was going on. A red flag would have meant a foul; a white flag meant a legal jump. I was so relieved when I saw that white flag!

"That's over twenty-eight feet!" I would learn later that Ralph told British long jumper Lyn Davies, who questioned,

"With his first jump? No, it can't be." The crowd was still on its feet, athletes and fans running down on the field, showering me with kisses and hugs. Ralph and Charlie Mays walked around the perimeter with me as we waited for the results of the jump. What was happening is that the Olympic officials were faced with a state-of-the-art electronic optical device that did not measure more than twenty-eight feet! They had to send someone out of the stadium to purchase a measuring tape. I knew none of this at the time. So I waited and waited and waited. My nerves were tangled in the pit of my stomach.

Finally, after a twenty-minute delay, and several measurements taken to validate the results, the result: 8.90 meters, flashed up on the scoreboard. "What does that mean?" I asked Ralph. He told me that it meant I had jumped twenty-nine feet two and one-half inches!

"He has made us all look like children!" Igor lamented in his heavy Russian accent.

It was more than I had ever dreamed of! I had just smashed the Olympic and world records by almost two feet! All that emotion, those years of rejection, disappointment and confusion that had been sublimated into push-ups and sprints up mountains and bounding drills and visualization, flooded my psyche and were transformed into tears and nausea. I felt as though I was between time and space. My legs collapsed under me and I slid down to the ground with Ralph holding my right arm and Charlie my left. Was I going to wake up and find myself back in South Jamaica in jail busted for armed robbery or something? Was this really real? Was I here? Later, Lyn would tell Ralph that he could not go on, what was the point, that I had destroyed the event. Me!

Gloria emerged from the crowd and we hugged each other so tightly that we could not speak. Dreams do come true, Bob Beamon. I had the audacity to still believe that. All across the world, ABC Sports beamed out the medal ceremony. When the "Star Spangled Banner" played and the flag began to rise, I stood at the highest level of the victory stand, a gold medal hanging from a green grosgrain ribbon around my neck. My warm-up pants legs were rolled up exposing my black socks. It was my statement of solidarity with the cry for help that Tommie and John had made. Klaus Beer of East Germany stood to my right wearing a silver medal. Barefooted and proud in his silent demonstration of solidarity, Ralph Boston, the man who had inspired me to be an Olympian, stood tall wearing his bronze medal. I had broken his records. It was awkward for both of us. But as a champion, he was gracious and supportive of my victory. He knew how hard I had worked, and he may have understood just how much I wanted it.

As the national anthem came to its final bars, I looked at the flag. I was in a daze. My stare was blank as I asked myself, *Where do I go from here?* I knew that the flag that stood for freedom and democracy did not stand for me. As I walked away from the victory stand and waved to the cheering crowd, a light rain began to fall. The lukewarm rain seemed to sober me a bit but I was still dazed.

Gloria and I went back to the villa and then we dressed in our best outfits. Mel and his wife took us to a romantic restaurant for dinner. The next day I rested and enjoyed being with Gloria, but it was as if I was still not of this earth. I couldn't help but wonder, even if for only a second, if I had not had sex the night before, would I have jumped thirty feet?

Then I got antsy. It was time to break the trance. I had to get back to El Paso and study for midterms. I had been gone for almost four weeks. I had to keep up in school or end up classified 1A, which meant death to me, shipping out to Viet Nam status. Many, many guys in my neighborhood had come home in body bags. I wanted to have a chance for an education so that I would be in a position to scrutinize the opportunities that were likely to come my way as an Olympic champion. I had to leave Mexico City before the closing ceremonies. I had to leave Gloria and return to god-awful El Paso. I had to switch focus. I had given all I had to the Olympics. I had given all I had to Gloria. She was hurt because she had to go back to New York and I had to go back to El Paso. I had been promising her for over two years that I was going to get a divorce from Melvina. I was hurt because I loved her. I promised her again that now that the Olympics were over I would do it.

People ran after me for autographs at the Mexico City airport, and the luggage handlers chanted "Beamon! Beamon!" as I walked by them. *Man, what an honor,* I thought, *this must be how Muhammed Ali feels when people chant, "Ali! Ali! Ali!"* Then I boarded the plane and settled in my seat for the flight to El Paso.

* * *

When the American Airlines DC-9 landed, I straightened my suit, anticipating more attention. I climbed down the portable stairs and walked across the asphalt landing field toward the terminal. Large balls of tumbleweed rolled in the dust close to my feet. A familiar hollow feeling shot in my gut.

Not one person spoke to me as I waited at the baggage-claim area for my luggage. When I collected my bags, I hailed a taxi and went directly to my house. I tried to allow myself to hope that Melvina was still in Mexico. My heart felt empty and alone, but when I felt the gold medal in my right pants' pocket, my emotions became so mixed—the agony and the ecstasy.

I had just enough money to pay the cabdriver, five dollars and a quarter out of six. I walked to the front door and opened it with my key. Ah, she was not there. Then, I dropped my bags and turned on the television to ABC, to watch the events of the day. Had I really been there at the Olympics? Had I just performed what people called the most remarkable feat in athletic history? The jump that was named Beamonesque. Had I? As I watched the Olympic wrap-up on television, my jump shown over and over, listened to endless discussions and commentary on how and why I jumped that far, and saw my team-mates, John and Tommie and Al and Dick and Lee and Larry and Ron, I wondered again, *Where do I go from here?* My question lulled me to sleep as the television's sign-off signal hummed in the dark empty space of my living room.

Chapter Eight

Imagine

Back then, I didn't know a damn thing about the Masons and Eastern Stars. Only thing that I can recall is that Ma wanted me to be a part of this collective of socially correct black folks. Seems that a black fellow named Prince Hall was the initiator of the Masons movement in the United States. He brought the concept from England to Connecticut before anyone else—white or black.

Anyway, the Eastern Stars are the female support arm of the Prince Hall Masons. There, Ma and I were sometimes caught between a flurry of mysterious handshakes and gestures that meant something to everyone but me. I really don't know how Ma fit into this equation since her husband, brother, son or father had to be a Mason, or her sister, mother or grandmother had to be an Eastern Star. Those were the rules. I wasn't up for all that stuff when I was a little kid. From the day when she told me she wanted me to become a Mason, I avoided being around on the evenings when she had meetings. She'd just have to go without me.

Hindsight is usually clearer than today's vision because when you are in the thick of things you sometimes can't see the forest for the trees. Knowing what I know now, I probably could have used some secret handshakes and secret codes to help me out of some of my predicaments. But who thinks of those things beforehand? I don't think I ever gave much thought to personal and political issues then. That is why there is such truth to the saying "knowledge is power."

To be honest with you, I didn't know what to think. I knew how to run, jump, train for basketball and track, dance, play the drums and fornicate. I knew how to push my mind and spirit so that my body would respond. I knew how to make a female scream when I was aroused. Damned if I knew anything about pushing my mind and spirit so that my heart would respond. I couldn't relate to that. I had glimmers of emotions that made me smile and kept me warm, but I had no experience to which I could compare or measure them.

I was called a "rare talent" by *Track & Field News*, which named me Athlete of the Year in 1968. Coming behind a double victory in the long jump and triple jump at the *San Francisco Examiner* Track & Field Meet in San Francisco, I was the overwhelming choice of the judges: seventeen out of twenty-three.

There were scientists who analyzed my jump using the laws of physics, discussing velocity, trajectory and aerodynamics, among other things. Then there were others who analyzed my performance and my life based on their personal slant of racial disdain. They played the race card when they said that I jumped that far because I was black. After all, they said, blacks have longer legs, thicker ankles and that our muscular make up is different. That's why they said blacks made good slaves: strong bodies with no brains. They called me superhuman and referred to me as a jumping machine. But, thank God, everyone did not and does not think like that. Even today, I have people come to me all the time and tell me that they have studied the scientific analyses of my jump in their college classes.

And the other point of view? I acknowledge it as hateful and dangerous and I no longer allow it to taint my perception of my accomplishment.

Today, I have placed all that speculation in its proper perspective. Then, however, I was numb from it. What I had done was what any athlete worth his or her salt would have done. I figured out during my training and competition that I needed to work on my speed to take my performances to another level. So when I jumped from the board I had speed. Speed. Not black speed or white speed—just speed.

I realized that some track-and-field people and reporters thought of me as some kind of freak. So I was expected to put on a freak show at every competition. Superhuman they called the jump. But the man who jumped was very human, even though he did fly.

For the next three track meets, I ran for the Houston Striders, the same track club that I represented at the Olympic Games. I was recruited by Dave Rickey, who was a white Texan from Houston with a thick drawl who walked and spoke like the homeboys on my block. He wanted to make money and he wanted to make money off us, and we felt obligated to him. In the 1960s, a "white, black-acting man" had more of a chance of being accepted and trusted by many blacks. But Rickey was the promoter and we were the talent. In the world of track and field, the promoter always got paid and the athlete hardly ever got paid. It appeared that it was in the best interest of the "professionals of the sport" to keep the amateur status thing intact.

I was kicking butt at the track meets, yet I was working without a trainer. I was breaking each meet long-jump record by more than a foot and a few inches. The passion that had been in my heart for track and field began to dissipate with each passing day. I felt empty and alone.

"Beamon, you are behind on your car note again," the man from the bank said. "Aren't you suppose to be an international sports champion, or something? Seems to me that you can afford to pay your bills."

I heard that all the time. The impression was that I was rolling in money but the truth was I could hardly pay my bills, but I was expected to train and compete on a full-time basis. In 1969 there was no professional track and field. We could only

get paid expenses. There were a lot of under-the-table pay-
ments but nothing could be proven. Corporate contracts were
the only way to survive. It was like living between a rock and
a hard place: In order to be a world-class athlete the paying
spectators would want to pay to see perform required a full-
time commitment to stay in top competitive form. Of course,
the track-meet promoters always got paid very, very well.

I had a one-on-one with Jesse Owens at the Four Seasons
in New York in late 1968. I asked him if I should be thinking
about competing in the Olympics in 1972. He told me, "You
don't need to do another Olympics. You have already proven
your ability. I will help you in any way I can." I was relieved.
A couple of weeks later, I called him and I called and I called.
Mr. Owens never returned my phone calls to follow up on our
conversation. I still don't know why that happened but I will
always respect Jesse Owens as an Olympic champion.

He wasn't the only one who made promises he did not
keep. "Bob you should be pitching cars and doing commercials," I would be told by promoters, marketing executives,
strangers, people at cocktail parties, people at charitable
events—you name it. Even the know-it-alls from the neighborhood would have their two-cents say about what I should be
doing. Like I didn't know. Like I was sitting on my butt, or
something, missing all these great opportunities coming my
way. I collected business cards, made phone calls and waited
and waited and waited for my big break. I was promised jobs,
endorsements, advertisements, and I'd never hear from them
again. I was too polite and too unsure of myself to confront
these people directly and ask them, "What's going on with all
the work you promised me?" These people were always so
happy to see me and shake my hand and take a picture and get
an autograph. I would always oblige, signing, "Bob Beamon
29' 2 1/2" Mexico City 1968"—been autographing that way
since October 18, 1968. Someone told me back then that "Bob
Beamon gave significance to the measurement twenty-nine

feet, two and one-half inches. Without you what would those numbers mean? Just another set of digits." But as time was passing, I was beginning to ask myself, *What does twenty-nine feet two and one-half inches and a world and Olympic record really mean?*

I was dizzy from being put on hold and then told that they were sorry that Mr. So-and-So couldn't take my call right now and could I leave a number? Sometimes I would ask to hold on if they said Mr. So-and-So was on another call. They would sound annoyed about me hanging on the line—so I'd eventually hang up and then just call back five and six times a day. I was desperately seeking a break—any break. I was hoping that their promises were real.

"I'd like to help you, Bob, but how can a black man sell soap?" I was told by one corporate executive. You see, if one can imagine it, there were no black pitchmen for products and services in the advertising world during 1968 and 1969.

Then my phone rang one morning: "Bob Beamon, this is Dr. Flaschen from ITT. I want you to come to New York to meet with me." "Finally!" I yelled as soon as I hung up the phone. I was so excited I did not ask him any details, all I knew was that he was sending me a plane ticket to come meet with him. Me, meeting with a major player in a major corporation. I packed my bags, went to the airport, my ticket had been all arranged and I boarded that plane in first-class and I was on my way to New York City and ITT. Now, how about that? Once I boarded in Dallas it was nonstop to La Guardia.

When I arrived at LaGuardia, a driver was waiting to take me to the Plaza Hotel. Yes, first-class all the way. As the car exited the airport, I remember taking a deep breath and stretching my legs out as I watched the lights of Manhattan get closer and closer. Coming to New York was bittersweet for me. I did not look behind me to Queens. I had to look ahead to my destination and keep myself focused on the reason I was there. New York made my stomach burn and moan. Flashbacks of all

the emptiness, the poorness, the foolishness, flickered inside
my head like an ancient silent movie. Seemed like a cloud of
gloom would follow me whether I went back to my old neighborhood or not. It was enough for me to be in the area for anxiety attacks to erupt. All I wanted to do was leave. But leave
to go where? Back to the dusty desert of El Paso and to
Melvina? There was no going backward—for me my circumstances were unpleasant enough to forge me forward—because
it was uncomfortable for me to stay there. Isn't that how the
Creator sometimes forces us to make changes and move along?
We ignore the signs or procrastinate, knowing deep down in our
soul that we need to do something different, go someplace different, or be someone different.

When I checked into my room, I called room service and
ordered dinner—a well-done T-bone steak with a baked potato
and salad. Hot apple pie a la mode and coffee completed the
food orgy. I did not leave the room after that. I did not even
call Gloria. All I could think about was my new job with ITT
and being fresh and ready when I met with Dr. Flaschen in the
morning.

It took forever for the sun to rise. It took forever for 10:30
to come. The driver had rung my room about 10:00 and taken
me to Dr. Flaschen's office in mid-town Manhattan. For that
day, I wore a brown, three-buttoned English-tailored suit, white
shirt and coordinated silk necktie and matching handkerchief. I
had about twenty suits, most of them were given to me as trade
for appearances. I was the best-dressed broke man in New
York. I felt like a million dollars—and as you would expect, I
tried real hard to look like a million dollars. Finally, I was sitting in the reception area of his office, and, his assistant came
out to get me.

"Bob, good to see you. How was your trip?" Dr. Flaschen
greeted me. I was so focused on him that I did not see his two
young sons, ages ten and twelve, standing at his side. These
two kids had seen my jump and were full of questions. It was

great. I remember sitting in a leather tufted-back chair and feeling like I was flying. It was wonderful.

I was glowing. Only thing, I was careful how I smiled, because my front teeth were still missing and I was very conscious not to reveal the gaps. Then Dr. Flaschen, his sons and I rode the elevator down to the lobby. I said good-bye to the boys and walked with Dr. Flaschen to a little cafe a couple of blocks away.

During our lunch, he asked me about where I saw myself in the next five years. I told him that I saw no future for me in athletics. I told him about all the promises that had not materialized; that I wanted to move into some sort of career. You see, major corporations had begun to hire athletes as part of their public relations and community outreach departments.

Then he asked, "What is your degree in?"

And I answered, "Oh, I don't have it yet. I'm still working on it. But my major is speech and drama."

There was a long very uncomfortable silence for the first time during the entire three hours that we had been together. It was even more apparent because our conversation had just been so lively. Then he spoke, "I thought you would have graduated this year. Aren't you twenty-three?"

"No, not until August," I replied. "But I have two more years to go."

There was no doubt in my mind that something had gone amiss. Now the long gaps of silence covered the minutes from the end of the entrée to coffee; both of us passed on dessert.

The short walk back to the office seemed to take an eternity; it was awkward and coolly polite. As soon as the elevator doors opened and Dr. Flaschen saw his secretary, he told her to call my driver and that he could take me anywhere I wanted to go that afternoon.

Then he and I walked back to his office. He closed the door behind him and turned to me and said, "Bob, you need to finish college. That is the most important thing that you can do for yourself right now—and that is the most important thing I can tell you to do."

I nodded.

"Stay well and keep in touch," he said as we shook hands.

I guess I told him thank you. I guess. I was numb. I could have run down twenty-nine flights, jumped thirty feet and leaped small buildings in a single bound. Look up in the sky, it's a bird, it's a plane, no, it's just Super Bob. But what's happening? He's losing altitude. He's just crashed to the bottom of the earth. Once again.

The ride from midtown Manhattan to LaGuardia had never seemed that long before. I couldn't say that about the heaviness that I felt in my heart. I had felt that before; many, many times before. It must be normal for the heart to feel so thick, so loaded down, I rationalized.

I'm going to finish college. No matter what it takes, I'm getting my degree by any means necessary! I repeated the mantra in my head.

Back in El Paso, I was even more preoccupied with my classwork—which, of course, was a welcome distraction from my personal life with Melvina and my "family" back in Queens. And now, I also had two trouble-bound preteen boys living with me. Bert and Daddy asked me if my brother, Chris, and his friend could live with me and Melvina for a while. They needed to get out of New York since they were hanging with the wrong crowd and something bad was sure to happen if they stayed. How could I say no? On top of everything else, they were suffering from culture shock. They were used to concrete and subway trains. In El Paso they had pickup trucks and tumbleweed.

But this whole incident with Dr. Flaschen got me thinking and remembering. I started mentally training for another competition. But this time it was for an education.

I recalled one of my first memories of having a dream or a goal to shoot for: that summer when I won the long-jump competition in the Junior Olympics at Randall's Island when my picture ended up in *The Daily Mirror*. I remembered dreaming I would become an Olympian after I saw Ralph Boston, Wilma Rudolph and Donna DeVarona. I had dreamed that I would go to college, that I would have a happy and loving family life. So my dream of winning the Junior Olympics came true. My dream of becoming an Olympian came true beyond what I had initially imagined. My dream of going to college came true. But my dreams of personal happiness kept eluding me. Like tacking Jell-O to a wall.

"Ma, I'm so unhappy being with—" and before I could finish my sentence she would cut me off.

"Be quiet! Don't be stupid. That girl loves you!"

It was an impossible situation. I trusted that Ma knew what was best for me. Even though my gut tossed and turned in tormented restlessness day in and day out.

My house was not my sanctuary. Absolutely not. I went "home" when I had nowhere else to go, when I was so tired and exhausted or hungry. In that respect I did not stand up for myself. I was focused on "doing the right thing," according to Ma. I had blind faith when it came to Ma. She would lead, I would follow—and I accepted that.

I was emotionally exhausted: All these emotions were circling around me with no place to settle because I only recycled them and never dealt with them head-on. Like I said, I had Melvina, Chris, Ma, Gloria, El Paso, UTEP, being famous in some circles—especially when I'd travel to Europe to compete—meeting and greeting with heads of state, kings and queens, corporation presidents and winning track meets and the media. The promoters were getting wealthier and wealthier. Promoters from Germany, Italy, France, Spain, you name it, always had some kind of barter proposition for me to compete in their event. I went for the exposure, the travel and the experience. And to be honest, I needed to hear cheers when my name was called especially after having all the rejection in my own country.

But as is written, God works in mysterious ways. I survived the abusive childhood, the gangs, the ridicule, the alternative school, by always blocking out the pain and focusing inward to achieve my goals—whether it was finally learning how to read at fourteen or training like nobody's business to be the best in basketball and in the long jump and triple jump.

There were several times when the demons from the past would rear their ugly heads and try to entice me into "more lucrative enterprises of the streets."

"You know, Bobby, you could invest in a few kilos of 'H' and walk out like a big dog," suggested a voice from the past.

"It's a damn shame a champion like you should have money problems. You know, though, that brothers got to do what the brothers got to do. That other shit is for the white boys," that voice haunted me.

Don't think I didn't consider such temptations, even if for a moment, as I watched my bills stacking up and the pressure to compete becoming more intense. Trying to juggle a real academic schedule with the kind of training schedule necessary to keep my body in competing shape (I continued to be my own coach and trainer) was wearing me down. The demons' voices grew from whispers to clear, convincing ideas. Then I would shake them away and battle inside. *I can do this. I can make it without going back to the gutter.*

It was December 1968, scholarship money was running thin and I got an invitation to meet the President of the United States, Lyndon B. Johnson, to receive an award. Melvina drove me to the airport. I had less than five dollars in my pocket. There I sat on the dais with the President at an Urban League affair in Houston. I had no idea how to make small talk. I sat between Mrs. Brown, an official from the Urban League, and the President, frozen with uncertainty about what to say and how to say it. Mrs. Kiska's public speaking sessions helped me when I had to make a formal speech, but I was lost when it came to one-on-one conversations.

But that was only the beginning of my horror that night. Initially I was so relieved when the waiters started serving the main course. *Thank God. Now I can have an excuse for not talking—because I have to eat—can't do both, now can I?* To my dismay, the main course was fried chicken. Here I was, dressed to kill in a tailored black tuxedo with satin lapels (from that shop in Mexico), self-tied bow tie, five dollars in my pocket and my stomach bubbling and groaning from anxiety. *How do I eat this chicken leg?*

"You better go 'head and pick up that chicken leg and eat it," Mrs. Brown whispered in my ear. I grinned, slightly, embarrassed but relieved at the same time. I picked it up and took a bite, then another. Those were the only bites I had all evening. The program continued and I was called up to receive an award. President Johnson extended his hand and looked at my shoulder instead of in my eyes. He told me, "Good job," and out of no where, I said, "I need a job." He looked startled and his people moved me along—and we all smiled and grinned appropriately for the cameras. The ceremony was over and I didn't know how I was going to get to the airport or how I was going to pay my car note that week.

Since I had become recognized as a world-class athlete, lots of people were smiling in my face. Should I have probed deeper to discover what was behind those smiles? I hadn't a clue. Instead I just absorbed it all. I took those smiles personally. Who were they smiling at? Me? No one had ever smiled at me like that before. I thought that they were just nice people who liked me. I had no sense of what being a "celebrity" meant to other people.

What it meant to me was that more people now knew my name, so I would have opportunities to make a decent living using my own persona. Corporations would pay me to promote their products, speak to their sales force, inspire schoolchildren on their behalf. Man, finally, I thought I'd be able to contribute in a big way and help myself and my family in the process. After all, the guy who took my photograph at the Olympics did.

Tony Duffy was a part-time photographer and a full-time accountant from England. He was there in Mexico City near the sandpit when I leaped. He captured me in a frontal pose while I was still in midflight. My photographic image was the one that started Allsport Photography, a multimillion-dollar company. It made Tony Duffy a millionaire. Tony has since sold his interest to Steve Powell and Allsport Photography continues to be the premiere photographic documenters of the top sporting events in the world. Go figure.

If Tony could use my persona and make a living, surely *I* could use my persona to make a living. Right? Not exactly.

I won't lie to you. I never purported to have an eagle eye for business. But I truly expected that someone with integrity and knowledge would see the potential in me and offer to put it all together for me. Right? Not exactly.

Melvina was all over me. I hated to go to my house. Calling it home would be stretching it a bit. Most of the time, I'd be in the campus library staring at pages I had already read a hundred times or just walking and thinking—mainly just stalling for time hoping that she would be in a deep sleep when I got there. But I'd be exhausted and I had to go to sleep some time.

Ma was absolutely no help to me. Here I was struggling with the naive concept of an *Ozzie and Harriet* marriage that I had repeatedly played in my head. No way did I want a marriage like Ma had or my mother had, or Daddy. I wanted to be swept off my feet by love for a beautiful woman who spoke to me in sweet tones. Her scent would follow her into the room. Oh yes, I was a romantic, but somehow I was precluded from happiness; frozen into a pattern of helplessness in my personal life. I knew I was in love with Gloria but I couldn't/wouldn't leave Melvina to be with her. I probably thought I knew whom I loved, but I really did not know what love was. I only knew what it wasn't. I look back at that scenario now and I see how my low expectations for my personal happiness were based on the low expectations of those in Jamaica, Queens who comprise my memories of the first decades of my life.

I did not define my inner power outside of athletics. I wanted a college education. I did not have the desire to compete anymore. I felt let down by the sport and its people; nevertheless I refused to languish in self-pity. My way of handling disappointment was simply to move on. I did not know why people speculated so much about me. I was quiet and mostly kept to myself. I had my own style: Even when I jumped some writers called my way "erratic." Some writers called my fashions "flamboyant." I hated that word. It reminded me of a pimp or someone gaudy. Yet, Daddy always told me that the only time I should dress like someone else should be when I am in a uniform. He said I should develop my own style—to stand out from the pack. Well, I did not think that an English-tailored pinstripe suit with a carnation in the lapel was flashy in an era when bell-bottoms, platform shoes, and felt fedoras with feathers were in vogue.

"You look so elegant, sir," a waiter said as I gave him my order, "You dress like they do in Europe."

"Thank you."

People often mistook my quiet nature and uncertainty of expression as arrogance. There I was thrust into a calvacade of cameras with reporters shouting questions I did not know how to answer properly. I was a babe in the woods; naive, immature, unprotected and willing to please. But I never said much. For example, I was asked why I went all the way to a track meet in Europe not to compete but just to profile at sidewalk cafes. It never occurred to me that they were taking digs at me. I never thought to explain that I had been injured and that the promoters begged me to come and just walk around and wave to the crowd. After all, Bob Beamon defied gravity and I felt my being injured was just not what they wanted to hear.

I didn't know what was going on in this new world of celebrity in which I suddenly found myself. Spiritually, I had no concrete values, though I'd had glimpses and flashes of Scripture and gospel lyrics when Ma and Daddy use to take me to church and Sunday school. I had not learned how to apply the concept of going inside myself for answers. I did not realize that I could have applied the same principles I used in athletics—visualization, mantras, belief—in my personal life as well. One was apples and the other was oranges. It wasn't until much later that I learned that our power from within is to be used for everything in our lives.

After the Olympics, I was different in many ways. I heard philosophers say that the beauty of life is to be enjoyed during the journey, not necessarily at the destination. And that's what I felt. I reviewed all the energy I had put into training and being the best, how I managed to overcome the loneliness and the personal temptation to stay put and not to grow. I thought of Ma, my staunchest ally, pushing me into marriage and then telling me that I need to get a job and forget all that college stuff. I remembered my stupidity in trying to negotiate my own college deal. All this I had gotten the better of so that I could change my life; and I see that I'm still a nigger, ghetto ignorant and charmingly gullible. Is this all there is? That dash between your birth date and your death is what really matters.

A group of businesspeople from El Paso and New York City, including Mrs. Manchuca and Mrs. Kiska, donated or raised money that semester for the nine former team members, who refused to compete with Brigham Young, to continue attending UTEP.

I kept singing that Dionne Warwick song to myself, "How Many Days of Sadness." I wanted and needed to get out of El Paso for my own sanity. But the business group was paying our tuition to demonstrate their disdain for our expulsion because of the Brigham Young incident. Plus, if I wasn't a student then I'd get drafted to Viet Nam and the odds were definitely in the favor of me being put in the infantry and on the front line. Those were the positions that went with black maleness. Muhammed Ali said, "Ain't no Viet Cong ever called me a nigger."

You could say I was disillusioned about the Olympics and the racist double standards in the United States. Growing up, television had been a major escape from the rawness of poverty, but there was also the in-your-face wake-up call: Beaver and Wally, Ricky and Dave didn't look like me—only Buckwheat, Stymie and Farina did, and they dressed like hell! Even for an intelligent man, those constant images were adversive. If I were white and had no other exposure to blacks outside of TV I would think negatively about them. So being black these negative images frustrated and disgusted me. Damn, it was hard enough getting ahead without this kind of propaganda saturating the airwaves and print about black people.

I mean, after all, black people did not create the sundown laws in Mississippi that prohibited blacks from walking the streets in the white sections of town after sundown, or the grandfather clauses that kept blacks from owning property or voting, or the policies that barred white insurance companies from writing policies to protect homeowners or their health and life. They didn't tell the banks to refuse to accept black customers or if they accepted their deposits to refuse homeowner loans to them. Economic racism is the glue that politically, and at one time legally, favors one race of people over another. So it's not in my mind or a figment of my imagination. Just like when my father-in-law, Willis Wilson Walter, Sr., fought in the U.S. Army's segregated anti-aircraft unit in Germany in World War II and the German bombers shredded his head and back with shrapnel. The medics fought intensely to stop the bleeding and he needed a transfusion to survive. But the Red Cross separated black blood from white blood and they were out of black blood for his blood type. Thank God for a Jewish doctor who said, "To hell with this shit," and took the blood that this

American soldier needed from the white blood bank. Anyway, being challenged and questioned for just being alive has made me strong and caring, not weak and bitter. Next!

Bills were stacking up, and I was feeling the pressure of not having the personal allowance from the scholarship. Melvina's job helped to keep the lights on, the phone on occasionally, and food in the refrigerator. My brother, Chris, and his friend were still living with us. In the eyes of my family and neighborhood, *I had made it.* They did not have a clue. They thought I was rolling in dough. Of course, having them in El Paso made no sense. I was struggling myself, but then, I was not struggling like they were struggling—different levels of struggling.

I was tired. I was studying for midterms and competing at the same time. My tutoring sessions were helpful but it just took me longer to absorb the information because of so many distractions. This was when those basic fundamentals of learning that I missed in elementary and middle school really caught up to me. Nevertheless, I was determined to finish college.

It was time to go on the road again. Just a week after the double victory in San Francisco, I was off to Washington, DC, for a major track meet. I was rushed, I was tired, and I missed the connections because the plane was late leaving El Paso.

When I got to DC, I hardly had time to sleep, let alone warm up correctly. My body was tight and tense as I stood on the runway ready to make my jump. Then, I accelerated and I heard it. *POP!* It was loud and definite. It sounded like the stereo version of a whip snapping. It was my left leg as I landed in the sandpit during my first try at the meet.

Chapter Nine

What's Going On?

The jump was good enough to win the meet, in spite of what had just happened. I limped off the track and was astonished as the crowd stood up and applauded me. I waved to acknowledge my appreciation as I held the pain behind my closed-mouth smile. My only thought was to put some ice on it.

Coming off the track, I saw Ron Bazil who had been my health teacher at Jamaica High.

"Mr. Bazil, what arc you doing here?" I asked.

"I am a dean at Adelphi University, Bob. You pulled that hamstring pretty bad, huh? It is the worse kind of pain, isn't it? You better take care of that right away."

"Yeah. It's nothing. I just need to stay off it for a little while."

"I heard about the problems at UTEP. If you want to come home and finish your education I could help you get a scholarship. You wouldn't even have to compete unless you wanted to. Call me," he said, and passed me his card.

He sure did lay something on my mind.

* * *

There are two Zen sayings: "Lessons are repeated until they are learned," and "When the student is ready the teacher will appear." They give some simple clues to solving this mystery we call life. But if one does not understand the concept of life as a journey of lessons, then these words have little meaning. And as for *moi*, I was lost when it came to the big picture. But something was guiding my soul through the fire.

I was struggling without the scholarship money I depended on to pay bills and buy food. But Mrs. Manchuca had raised the money to enable me to go to a dentist and have a bridge fitted for my mouth. I had been missing all my upper front teeth since I was fourteen. I cannot tell you how much I appreciated her doing that for me. Now I could talk and smile freely without using my hand to cover my mouth when I spoke or smiled.

Smile or no smile, I had to make some serious decisions about my future. What on earth was I going to do next?

Don Haskins was the basketball coach at UTEP. He offered a scholarship to me if I would play on the team. He made it clear—I would not be in the starting lineup.

"If you join the team, you are going to play Don Haskins' basketball," he said.

To be sure, he was the star of the UTEP coaching staff. He was the one to whom UTEP attributed their financial success— through their nationally acclaimed basketball team.

It was Haskins who recruited all "the brothers" from the big city housing projects to play ball for him. Haskins' ego was bigger than the state of Texas!

As much as I would have loved to play on the same team as Nate "Tiny" Archibald, I felt the last thing I needed to do to myself at this time was to set myself up to fail. Haskins' approach simply offended me. His style of coaching was confining, abrasive and military-like. He wouldn't hesitate to call a player "stupid." I needed a scholarship but not at any cost. Bottom line was that I wanted the hell out of El Paso.

I knew very little about being injured. I'd never had anything more than a cramp before this hamstring pull. Although I was competing under the Houston Striders Track Team banner, I didn't have a coach or trainer. I was mostly there in name only. And, though I wasn't competing well, they used my involvement to attract other athletes. I wasn't making any money, either. This hamstring injury was making it more and more difficult for me. My leg was weak, so I lacked the confidence I needed to predict how it would respond when I took off from the runway or landed in the sandpit. Sort of like when you rise from a sitting position you have an automatic expectation that your legs will have the strength to hold your body upright. It became more difficult day in and day out. I couldn't find the right treatment to rehab that leg. It never did heal right. I started to feel really bad about not being able to perform. That injury became a very, very difficult thing for me to overcome emotionally as well as physically.

So I went to see Benny Tobin. He was the trainer for the UTEP Miners football and basketball teams, mostly. Benny told me to sit in the whirlpool a while every day. I did it twice. It felt better and I went on to the next meet to compete.

Big mistake. I should have sat it out until I was stronger.

"Look, Bob, all you have to do is show up and wave to the crowd. The press has been calling wanting to know if you'll be here. You know, your fans, especially the kids, will be so disappointed if you don't come. You won't have to jump, Bob—we'll let everyone know in advance that you are still injured. It'll be fine. Now, can I count on you?" a promoter asked.

You know what I did? Well, first of all I needed the expense money. But I felt so badly about just showing up and not competing that I jumped. I should've sat my butt down.

I came in second place behind an unknown competitor. Now that I was no longer just a noun but an adjective, "Beamonesque," that kind of performance was totally unacceptable.

Then in another meet I jumped on the right leg and still won the competition, even though the left leg was my jump leg. So I became ambidextrous-like with my legs. I was just trying to keep myself busy competitively. But the sports media seemed to select and report only the meets where I faced trouble.

They had a field day with me. They still called me inconsistent and erratic: I always jumped on my left leg—most long jumpers jump on their right leg—now I was jumping on the right leg and they still weren't satisfied. The truth was I didn't know how to say no to them, I didn't know when to sit down and shut up and I didn't know it was impossible to please everyone.

Although, thanks to Mrs. Kiska and Mrs. Manchuca, I was well spoken, I wasn't overly talkative. I was and am basically a quiet person who found it difficult to express himself. The media perceived me as conceited, cold, standoffish.

I had practice making speeches and doing cold readings from "Lilies of the Fields." But I did not have a clue how to handle reporters who appeared to have turned hostile toward me.

I was fed up with this kind of treatment—but it made me want an education even more. I began to wonder who were these people who have been given a license to judge? Suppose the spotlight was reversed?

* * *

"Mr. Bazil, this is Bob Beamon. Is your offer for me to come to Adelphi still good?"

"Just come, Bob. All you'll have to do is go to class and do your academic work. If you want to do anything else, the rest is up to you."

"Mr. Bazil, I don't want to compete. I just want to finish college."

"I'll discuss it with Dean Walker and we'll see what we can work out for you, Bob."

That's all I needed to hear. The rest was simple.

Adios, El Paso.

I had my wings back. God sure does work in mysterious ways. Deans Walker and Bazil arranged for me to attend school on a special scholarship. I was even assigned a counselor. I hated leaving Mrs. Manchuca and Mrs. Kiska but they were happy for me to have such a great opportunity. Their fundraising efforts and the donations had begun to dissipate. I had no desire to end up drafted for the Viet Nam War with a 1A classification.

Melvina moved into a house in Queens her mother had helped her buy. I was still stuck in many ways on material things and Melvina knew how to dangle that carrot in front of my face. I loved having the stereo equipment and just being able to say that I had a house. I hadn't had anything before. To have was a status symbol for this poor boy from Queens. But that situation was still too much for me to digest even with "the things." Besides my grandmother constantly reminded me that Melvina was good for me. I moved into a dormitory on campus and attempted "to will" that situation away. I submerged myself in campus life at Adelphi University.

I became fascinated with the work of anthropologist Margaret Meade. My counselor helped to identify a major that would suit me. I declared cultural anthropology as my major. I decided to join the track team and the basketball team, where I was a starting forward.

I was protected from the flak of Melvina by submerging myself in campus life. She and I had hardly anything in common. However, she had the power of my grandmother over me. I would call Ma sometimes and I would begin to tell her how unhappy I was with Melvina. She would always cut me off and tell me to shut up. It was the strangest thing. Like she and Melvina had some sort of secret bond or something.

I hardly saw Melvina while I was at Adelphi—hardly ever. Gloria was pretty much out of the picture by now. I guess she got tired of all my unkept promises; Gloria married someone else. Did I really love Gloria as much as I thought I did? Was I mature enough to know what love was then?

Stuart Dick was my psychology professor. He was Jewish, in his thirties, very observant, hip and a man who favored social and political liberties for all. He was very much a man of the 1970s, and very much into the study of the mechanism of human behavior.

He gave us a book list to select from. As I looked down the list, one title just froze inside my head, *Man's Search for Meaning*, by Viktor E. Frankl. He was a psychiatrist and a Holocaust survivor. An odd choice for a black man? Hardly.

I marveled as I read how Frankl, as a prisoner, endured the horrific concentration camps of Auschwitz and Dachau. He created the new theory of logotherapy out of his own painful experiences. Logotherapy, in simple terms, "focuses on the meaning of human existence as well as on man's search for such a meaning."

I couldn't put the book down. I couldn't stop turning the pages. I read how, while he stood in line for a morsel of food with other prisoners whose severely emaciated bodies resembled walking corpses, he would mentally and spiritually take himself out of that situation and focus on numbers or equations, or an imagined story. He clung to the memory of his beloved wife and lived with her in his inner life, created by head and heart. He did this for hours, for days, for months, for years. Somehow he found hope despite the hopelessness and cruelty that surrounded him. He had one kind of dream, but he lived another kind of life.

I thought about how I kept to myself for years. How I didn't ask questions and attempted to remain invisible in my house when I was growing up. In my head I had created an inner life of family and love, like I saw on *Ozzie and Harriet*. I had one kind of dream but lived another kind of life.

Then I got to this part:

We must never forget that we may [find meaning in suffering]. For what matters is to bear witness to the uniquely human potential at its best, which is to transform a personal tragedy into triumph, to turn one's predicament into a human achievement. When we are no longer able to change a situation...we are challenged to change ourselves.

(Frankl, Viktor E., *Man's Search for Meaning.* New York: Washington Square Books, 1984, p. 135.)

My life danced in front of me like a series of frenetic images. After I read Frankl's words, I saw those god-awful shoes that I had to wear to class; I recalled the show-and-tell fiasco, the gang, the time I slammed the teacher against the blackboard, Daddy knocking me down, Bert slapping me all around, and that damn Mr. Moore and his blackjack. I saw me with a noose around my neck. I shook myself out of my daydream.

Not only did Viktor Frankl write about the meaning of life, the meaning in suffering, but he wrote about the meaning of love. I remember absorbing every word. I was fascinated by the fact that I was even interested. But perhaps the timing was right for me to take the time to find answers. I guess I needed to be still for a minute in order to have clarity. It was similar to the experience when I was in training—solitary and focused—when the only thing on my mind was "seeing" my perfect jump. I didn't hear anything else. I didn't see anything else. That was my inner life then.

There just seemed to be so much I didn't know about life. Put me on a track or on a basketball court and I felt connected and confident. Take me out of that milieu, I was a blind man feeling my way without a Seeing Eye dog or a cane. Also, I was a man with an ego—I wasn't going to reveal my vulnerabilities. Shit, I had to halfway look like I knew what I was doing and where I was going. You know, it's a male thing. Like when we are lost and we refuse to stop and ask for directions: We would rather ride and ride as long as it takes to figure out what streets to take. Don't need to ask for directions.

Frankl's book had a profound effect on me. This is what he wrote about the meaning of love:

Love is the only way to grasp another human being, in the innermost core of his personality. No one can become fully aware of the essence of another human being unless he loves him...he sees which is potential in him...[b]y making him aware of what he can be and of what he should become, he makes these potentialities come true.

(Frankl, Viktor E., *Man's Search for Meaning*. New York: Washington Square Books, 1984, p. 134.)

I received an A in Stuart Dick's class.

Seemed like signs for me to probe the meaning of love and life were all around me.

One of my classmates gave me Hermann Hesse's *Siddhartha*. It was a thin book, a fable about an East Indian named Siddhartha who was searching for the key to life. Through a series of adventures, including acquiring material wealth and losing it, he discovers the answer to his question: The key is love; without love life has no true meaning.

I opened up to Warren Smith who taught Black Studies. I told him that I was so unhappy and I wanted a divorce. I admitted to him that I had become accustomed to the material comforts that Melvina provided: a stereo, television, a nice house; she was financially self-sufficient.

"Bob, do not become a prisoner of material things. Material things will come and go. You must never allow yourself to be compromised by them," Warren said.

But that was easier said than done. Hell, I had grown up yearning for things; stole them when I could. Deprivation overemphasizes the importance of the missing thing. People talk about trade-offs. What Warren Smith was telling me was to make decisions based on the source, the pure heart, never mind the trade-offs—the material temptations that can, and do, imprison you, if you allow them.

It was 1972. I was twenty-six years old. I graduated from Adelphi University with a Bachelor of Arts in Cultural Anthropology. In 1969, I had been the NBA's 15th-round draft choice for the Phoenix Suns in a supplementary draft although I still had college eligibility left. I told the Associated Press that I would compete in track until I got $250,000 from Phoenix. End of story. A couple of years later I considered playing for the ABA's San Diego Matadors. Instead, I accepted the offer from Home Federal Savings & Loan in San Diego to work in their public relations department.

Everyone was thrilled about my prospects of playing professional basketball. Everyone except me, that is. It was like all your life you dream that you want something, then when you get it, you feel empty inside. I don't remember asking specifically to have a professional basketball career. But I sure did ask for opportunities for a better life.

I truly felt at that time that I had no future in sports. Not basketball, and certainly not track and field. There was no such thing yet as professional track and field.

I reported to the Matadors' camp. I stayed a week. My heart was somewhere else. I was a weak dribbler and a super-strong jumper. I had a lot of work to do in order to be able to make it, truly make it, and not be a bench warmer. At that point, I simply did not have the inclination or the desire to put my energies there. In hindsight? I did the right thing for me.

So I accepted the offer from the bank. San Diego was a lush paradise. Yes, it had the reputation of a conservative, quiet Navy town, but it was on the ocean, fertile with hundreds of shades of green grass and trees. I loved the Mediterranean architecture mixed with the Mexican influences; I loved the pastel buildings.

I rented a deluxe, one-step-below-luxury, two-bedroom furnished apartment. I bought a stereo. I would spend hours there entertaining myself or friends with my music. I had quite a collection by now: jazz, salsa and rhythm and blues.

I had a set of congas. You couldn't tell me nothing, I was in hog heaven.

I had to wear suits and ties to my job every day. Man, did I love to dress up. They called me a sharp dresser. I would represent Home Federal at Rotary Club meetings, United Way events, corporate lunches, receptions and dinners.

I had picked up a few social pointers over the years and I learned how to work a room. I was apolitical—didn't get involved in other people's politics. I had always been a strong team player and I just translated that attitude from the track and court to the boardroom.

I threw myself totally into my new life. I answered question after question about how I did *it* and what I felt after I did *it*. Everyone wanted to know about "the jump." I never knew how to handle all the attention gracefully. I'd feel awkward when people would look and stare like I was some kind of idol or something. Many would tell me where they were when I jumped and how I inspired them.

Speaking to people and groups made me high. I felt energized by their enthusiasm toward me. It made me realize just how much that hamstring pull had taken from me spiritually and emotionally and how much it affected how I thought about myself. It made me realize that those mean-spirited comments and reactions to me had pierced my self-esteem. In this new job, I started to see myself in a different light. Still, I was still looking outside myself for answers. But this experience of working in the financial community made me more and more aware of where I might find my new niche.

But I still could not put my foot down where Melvina was concerned. I told her I didn't want her there. She showed up anyway. I pleaded with Ma to hear my side. It was utterly futile.

This has been going on for over seven years now, I'd remind myself.

Why would she continue to force me to be with someone I didn't love and had never loved.

Now, those same old feelings came back again. My lovely home was no longer home, it was merely a place to eat, sleep and shower. She had been there about six months. I could not stand to live like that any longer. She couldn't even keep me for the sex anymore, which had worked in the past. I had not touched her for five months.

"I don't want you here. I want you to go back to New York," I said.

One day, while I was at work, she took my car and credit cards and left for New York with another man as her traveling companion. A month later, she called to tell me she was pregnant and that I was the father. I could not believe that she was trying that shit again. Especially since she knew by now that I could not have children.

I had taken a fertility test in Queens. I wondered why Gloria hadn't gotten pregnant and Melvina said she had. The results of the test were negative. The doctor explained that my sperm count was low. He attributed that to improper medical treatment when I was afflicted with the mumps as a child. He told me that I could not impregnate any woman.

Besides that, it was physically impossible, unless she and the Virgin Mary shared the same secret. I hadn't slept with the woman. But I didn't take any action to divorce her before she had the baby. I did not realize the legal consequences of not doing so. So in the eyes of the law, we were still married. And legally that meant that the child was born during our "marriage." Melvina put me on the birth certificate as the baby's father, knowing full well that I was not the father of her child.

I made the mistake of letting her get away with that—I

should have fought. But I was young, ignorant of the law, just getting my life and finances together, and I never thought about the deep and hurtful consequences such a charade would later have on the child and myself. The child grew up thinking that I was her father who had abandoned her—I resented that but I kept silent. As the years passed, I began to feel guilty because the girl was carrying my name. Somehow, I felt it was too late to change it. She never saw me that much. Plus, if I could avoid being in touch with Melvina for any reason, I did. I believe it was cruel of Melvina not to have told her daughter from the beginning who her father was—but then Melvina would have had to admit that I, Bob Beamon, was not the father of her daughter and she had been lying about this for years. But besides all that, it is the child who suffers when this kind of confusion is allowed to happen. I was wrong not to quash the lie in the early stages. I regret that she lived a lie for so long, but I know I did the right thing when I finally told her. Now she can go on with her life and perhaps seek out her father.

So much deception was going on between Melvina and Ma. I lost something for Ma because I felt betrayed, used and deeply hurt. I started thinking about how Ma had moved Melvina into our house and how she was so adamant about my being with her.

A conversation with my friend Sudie in 1985 opened a new line of thought for me.

"Did you say Melvina was from another country?" he asked.

"Yes."

"Well, Bob, didn't you know that when she married you she became a U.S. citizen?"

"Damn, that's right. I hadn't thought about that."

Maybe her mother paid Ma to let Melvina be with me.

"Bob, you were a champion even in high school. Melvina saw fame, fortune and citizenship, and you were her ticket, baby."

"Damn."

"But her plan to lock you in with a baby fell through—for medical reasons. Even at the end, she was still trying to have a reason to call herself Beamon."

I had wasted all those years. I finally filed for divorce in New York. She didn't contest or seek child support.

My God, I was finally free of a dark cloud that had blocked out my sunshine. When I took the step to end this marriage once and for all, I felt like I had sprouted wings. I knew I could fly. I felt so light, a ton of bricks had been lifted from my shoulders. I even thought briefly about competing in the 1972 Olympics. But it was just a fleeting thought.

At the S&L, I was learning about investments. I also learned about auctions that sold repossessed cars for way below the Blue Book value. I identified the Cadillacs as good, sturdy, dependable cars that kept their value pretty well for an American car, so I started buying them below Blue Book and selling them for profit. This was in addition to my job at Home Federal.

It was no secret that clothes were my weakness. So when an acquaintance approached me about investing in a men's fashion store, I did not hesitate to say yes. I figured if nothing else, it was a good investment because I would save money, I could buy my wardrobe wholesale.

* * *

"Bob, come and sit down for a minute. I want to talk to you," said Allen Reed, head of public relations at Home Federal. He continued, "You have been a valuable asset to us and we want you to grow with us—like family. We want you to enter our management-training program in September. This will give you an opportunity to move up like Miller Starks over there."

Miller Starks was a former Oakland Raider turned banker.

I thanked Allen for the opportunity, told him I would need a little time to think about it and headed straight back to my office. I shut the door, slid down in my high back leather chair, and stared out of the window, looking at nothing in particular. I felt a knot forming in my gut.

It was reflection time again. I finally cleared my life of Melvina. I was still working out and running at least three times a week. I was dating freely and enjoying myself. I hardly spoke to anyone in New York. Daddy had turned his life around and stopped drinking; he was a shoemaker. He had a new wife; her name was Ianstha.

I had just sent my younger brother, Tim, back to New York. I had tried to help him make something of his life. I used my contacts and got him into junior college. He had exceptional talent as a basketball player, but he preferred to waste it smoking dope all day, hanging out with thugs and murderers in New York. I thought a change of environment would expose him to an alternative lifestyle that he might adopt. However, I learned, "You can lead a horse to water but you cannot make him drink."

Tim came down to stay with me packing weapons and a hanger-on, Julian.

Instead of going to class, Tim would get high all day, smoking joints, drinking beer and sipping vodka. When I found out, I refused to tolerate that shit in my house, so I put him out.

Then, he comes back high on something, and kicks my front door off its hinges. I sent him back to New York. By now he and my brother Chris were constantly in and out of trouble and evidently in and out of jail—like a revolving door. Sister Nanette did not follow their course of self-destruction, but her environment seemed to clip her wings.

Back home, I was the ultimate success story: I was supposedly rich and famous. After all I had been on television and in *The New York Times*. That's famous to the folks in the neighborhood.

I decided that a career as a banker was not for me. I

declined Allen's generous offer. It was early 1975, I had been there for more than two years. Guess it was a sign that it was time to move on. I registered for graduate classes in counseling at San Diego State University.

I sustained myself for a while with my wholesale car business and the clothing store investment. I was unsettled though. I had gotten comfortable with the salary from the bank. I wanted to have a family. I wanted to have a wife. And I wanted to make money.

The desire for material things began to take center stage again.

I met a woman at the university, a social worker. She was from a wealthy family, and she was crazy about me. I liked her very much. Her wealth, I admit now, was also an attraction. Against the wishes of her family, she married me; the marriage lasted for less than a year. I was rich for five minutes. It was a cruel and stupid thing to do, for now I was the deceptive one. Funny how toxicity can be contagious. It is said that the people around us mirror us in some way and that is the hardest thing to accept.

I decided after that episode I could acquire wealth on my own.

Lessons are repeated until they are learned. There's no such thing in life as three strikes and you're out. You go until you get it right. And you take as many tries and as much time as you need. No mortal man can determine that for you. But this is hindsight genius; at the time I was too close to it, couldn't see the forest for the trees. I couldn't see through the cracked glass.

During that time, I was even coaching a long jumper named Arnie Robinson, preparing him for the 1976 Olympics. Arnie came home with the gold that year.

I'd coach athletes from time to time, but I didn't consider it a job. I did find a job as a counselor at Linda Vista Youth Center while I was still working on my master's degree.

They said I was brilliant in helping young people with their problems, and I know why. I was working with kids from the inner-city who reminded me of myself. I had a special connection. It was only my own family members I couldn't seem to help. I'm told that's too often the case. Sometimes those closest to you tend to be the ones who take your advice for granted.

I didn't need a book to tell me what abandonment felt like. I knew the urgent need to belong to someone or something when you're seven, eight, nine, ten, whatever. Surrogate "fathers" would appear in all shapes and sizes—dressed in gang colors and enticing young neglected boys to feel wanted and a part of a family. They knew how to get them. They had been there once. They knew about those secret yearnings inside. Didn't matter how tough and together they may seem on the outside.

The projects in San Diego may have been a bit cleaner but no brighter than the ones in New York. Did you know that the same architects who designed most of the public housing in this country also designed many of the prisons? They designed small windows; sunlight could hardly break through. Being poor and living in the projects carried a stigma that I was only too familiar with.

Frankie, Brodie and Anthony were the core group to break through. Just like it was when I was a Frenchmen, someone had to bless you before you could walk the streets unharmed.

I brought my congas to the center to help break the ice.

Anthony was an attractive, neat, well-groomed hoodlum who could really play basketball well. So I would play the congas as Anthony and the guys would shoot hoops. Just like they did at the Rucker's Tournament in Harlem. The brothers would be drumming while the players would be dunking. Kareem Adbul Jabbar played in the Rucker's when he was Lew Alcindor. There was this brother named "Helicopter" 'cause he would fly circles around his opponents. They played some exceptional basketball. And lest I forget "The Goat."

So anyway, I wanted to bring the same vibe to these guys in hopes that they would eventually open up. They would clown around. Anthony could sing a little bit and always had the girls cheering him on. Gangbangers always have girls all around them. They say it's a power thing. It's also a money thing. Gangbangers always had cash.

About a year had gone by and Anthony and I were communicating on another level. He had begun to confide in me. He wanted to do what I had done—break away from that gang lifestyle.

"I don't have the sports like you did, man, 'cause I ain't that good in school."

I told him that he didn't know what he could do because he had not focused on being anything but a bully and a thief. I urged him to put the same amount of energy on positive things so he would get positive results.

One evening I was at the center following up on some paperwork. Most of the staff was gone and there were a handful of kids putting away the volleyball equipment. Then, like a flash, I heard:

"Mr. Beamon, Mr. Beamon, hide me. Hide me. They're going to kill me."

It was Anthony shouting as he sprinted through the front doors like a meteorite. My instinct propelled me into action. He had grabbed my jacket, almost slid down to his knees, pleading for help. He was drenched with sweat and trembling from fear.

I grabbed him and demanded that he tell me the truth. He told me that he had tried to break free from the gang. Now, they were convinced that he was going to be an informant since he didn't want to be affiliated with them anymore.

Then in mid-sentence, like in slow-motion, about seven gang members led by Frankie and Brodie crashed through the door and yanked Anthony right out of my arms. He pleaded as they dragged him out the door. They put a gun to my head and told me not to move. They slammed the door behind them and held it closed from the other side. I ran to the rear exit to go help him, but I froze in mid-motion as I heard Anthony say in a strong, definite voice, "Kill me, motherfuckers. Just blow my fucking head off."

Bang. Bang. Pop. Pop. Pop. Then it was still—eerily still. I opened the back door and ran to the front of the building. The perpetrators had all scattered by then.

The only person left was Anthony—a human bundle sprawled in a pool of blood. Was this the only way for him to be free? Where was the meaning in his suffering? Where was the meaning in his life? Damn it!

I was still on my search for meaning. It was time to move on.

Chapter 10

Truth or Consequences

I remember my "Hollywood debut" only too well.

"Take one. Bob Beamon. Action," shouted the assistant director.

"Take two...three...four...five..."

I was making a cameo appearance in *Golden Girl*, a film starring Susan Anton and Robert Culp. Culp was very distant and sarcastic, criticizing me in front of the cast and crew for needing too many takes. But when his turn came, he messed up royally. I was snickering to myself as he fumbled a few lines— proving there is such a thing as divine justice. That was in the early 1970s.

I had done some television from time to time, although not nearly as much as I would have liked. I had been in the ABC, NBC and CBS booths at major track events offering my own brand of observations and commentary. I'd sit there next to guys like Jim McKay sporting my headphones and a network blazer. ABC's *Wide World of Sports* opened with an announcer saying in part, "the thrill of victory and the agony of defeat" illustrated by a montage of athletic performances. My Olympic performance was one of the scenes.

I was often a celebrity guest for the *Superstars Show*. In the late 1970s and early 1980s, the network would invite celebrity athletes to somewhere warm and tropical during the dead of winter to compete in bowling, obstacle course maneu-

vers and silly carnival games in order to produce a TV special.
I played with athletes such as Bubba Smith, Mean Joe Green,
Walt Frazier, and Earl "The Pearl" Monroe.

There was a time when I had to put on a life jacket to row
a boat in four feet of water—I can't swim! The guys never let
me live that one down.

In 1984, I had been the principal in a national Miller Lite
commercial. I was one of the Miller Lite All Stars for three
years. I thought I had finally made it in commercials.

"You know, Bob, you did a great job. You came off natural, relaxed and most important of all, believable," said the
director.

"Thanks very much. So you think I may have a future in
commercials?"

"I don't see why not."

It took three agents to put my deal together. When the dust
settled, I took home less than $10,000 on a $50,000 deal. It was
obvious that I was still a novice in this area. I was still learning.

Later that year, I ran into Julius Erving at LAX during the
1984 Olympic Games. Julius and I had played a little ball
together when we were in college. He was attending the
University of Massachusetts. I was going to Adelphi. He grew
up in Long Island. I remember the day when he whirled around
me and dunked past me like a human tornado. Now he was a
famous NBA star; even nicknamed himself "The Doctor"—
because he'd be there to "make a house call in your face" if you
weren't paying attention.

He asked me how I was doing and I told him I was doing
okay, just wished I could get more work.

"Do you know who you are, Bob?" Julius asked me.

He was telling me not to sell myself short and to keep who
I was in perspective. Now that I think about it, he probably
meant that I should surround myself with positive, motivated
people; people who want to make the best of their lives. At the

time, I thought I knew who I was, so I smiled and we shook hands. I never forgot his question—I just filed it away; I didn't really have an answer.

* * *

I was still struggling to get my love life together. Even after being free from Melvina, a happy relationship still eluded me. My second marriage to Amy was a complete disaster. Not only did I get married for all the wrong reasons, I ended up hurting her in the process.

We both left with scars. Her family detested me and the tension between us was fierce. They saw me as one of her save-the-world projects that she married. There could be no future there. She was too close to her family for her to be happy in the long term with this awkward arrangement. I was too preoccupied with her wealth and trying to counteract my limited exposure to her world. Things really happened for the best. There was no *Ozzie and Harriet* potential there.

After Amy, I continued to look for love in all the wrong places.

"I want to die! I want to die!" Nia screamed the morning after our wedding.

What the hell? What is wrong with this woman, I wondered. She was a beautiful Iranian woman with long black hair, thick eyelashes, as delicate as a porcelain doll, ranting and raging like a caged animal.

I had met her in San Diego, too. Nia had seemed to be a blessing in disguise. At the time, I had just discovered that Toy, the woman I loved, was bisexual. I had suspected that something was up with Toy. She was always whispering on the phone—so clandestine and secretive. The "other lover" was a woman! I had never encountered that before. In my shock and naiveté I reasoned that she was a beautiful-to-the-bone woman who could have any man she wanted. Why would she want to sleep with a woman?

They all seemed to be wearing masks, these women I welcomed with open arms into my space: Melvina, Toy, Nia and others. Was I wearing a mask, too? They do say that the people around you are mirror images of yourself in some way. Damnit. What way?

Toy broke my heart. She knew I was straight and that I was under the impression she was too. She should have told me she was "bi." After all, we weren't having a one-night stand. She had moved from New York several months before so that we could be together in San Diego, we had talked about marriage. I was serious about Toy. I was vulnerable. The next thing I knew, I was with another deceptive beautiful creature. It didn't occur to me then that their beauty was only skin deep. As do most people, I assumed that if a woman was beautiful on the outside, had a sweet tone, like Ma, that she was beautiful on the inside as well.

I used this same judgment in other facets of my life. People who showed me some sort of attention and were nice to me gained my trust. I had absolutely no sense of myself as a sought-after celebrity, no sense of self-worth, but it seemed everyone else did.

So here I was in Madrid, newly wed, with a wife addicted to amphetamines and anti-depressants. She had locked herself in the bathroom and threatened to take her life. I was numb with shock. Was this some kind of joke? She was a sheltered woman from a wealthy and close-knit Muslim family. I had even begun converting to Islam to be accepted as her husband.

To make a long story short, I sent her back to her family in San Diego so that I could fulfill my contractual commitments in Spain. I was traveling constantly all over the country. I needed to know that she was not alone and could not overdose on her pills while I was away.

In spite of my problems with my wife, that was one of the best years I had ever had. I was treated as a champion. I was compensated as a champion. My ideas were respected and I was received with crowds of fans seeking autographs and exposure. To the Spaniards of that time, I was their Michael Jordan.

I was under a one-year contract to be the promotional sports-and-fitness representative for the Galeria Presidia, one of Spain's largest retail chains. I always had great coverage from *AS Magazine*, a leading sports newspaper in Spain. I had known Miguel Vidal, their ace reporter for years; in fact, he had come to San Diego to write a feature story on me.

I had a most profound romantic experience when my tour took me to Granada. I had agreed to have a late dinner with a few people. I was enchanted. The restaurant was a cave nestled in the side of a hill, the inside illuminated by hundreds of candles. I could just imagine the Isley Brothers song, "Gypsy Woman" as dancers in full colorful gypsy skirts danced and danced to the strings of a trio of guitars. I felt a warm glow cover my skin.

I don't need a woman with me, I confirmed to myself. *I just need to be with myself.*

I had felt such bliss only once before: in Viareggio, Italy, when I was having dinner alone at a restaurant on the water. The moonlight glow on the still water settled my spirit and warmed my soul. I felt divine.

That night, I fell in love with love.

It was 1980, I wanted to stay in Spain and work for another year, but Galeria Presidia moved too slowly in executing another contract. I guessed it was time for me to go back. I was homesick for the States. I flew back to New York with the firm intention of finding out about my mother from Ma. I found out that Ma was staying in Harlem for a couple of weeks, house-sitting for a friend. So I went to see her and get the key to her apartment in Queens. That was when I found out about my mother and my biological father. Nia and I moved into the housing projects with my grandmother until I could find a place. The transition from Madrid to Queens was extremely difficult for me. Everyone knew me in Spain. Hardly anyone knew me in New York. It was as if I had fallen from space. After a couple of months, I found a place for us in Coney Island in Brooklyn. Toy heard I was back in New York and called me. During the conversation, she asked me if I still loved her. I told her yes. Nia was listening on the phone in the kitchen. I guess she heard me talking low and got suspicious. I had no intentions of going back to Toy, but Nia was completely unstable. I knew she had had an affair with an Arabian pilot and became pregnant by him. During one of her tantrums, she had told me that she aborted our "little black baby." I knew she was lying because I could not have children. What hurt most was seeing the disdain she had for me, like I was beneath her.

Nia packed her suitcases, called a cab and left. The next day, she called from her sister's house in Washington, DC, to say she wanted to come back.

"I think you'd better stay right where you are," I said, and hung up.

I was dissatisfied with living in Coney Island. It was still very nice, but I wanted something more out of my life. I had lived abroad, been intimate with wealth and prestige; I had flown on a private jet to Germany with General Alexander Haig, as a guest for an Olympic fundraiser. I had been the guest of the royal family of Monacco. I had been to the White House more than once, all in conjunction with the international Olympic movement. And I talked the part and dressed the part. I loved to wear beautiful, Euro-tailored clothes. I was still fit at 175 pounds. I had gained about twenty pounds since I competed. It was pure muscle on my six foot four frame.

Outwardly it seemed I didn't have a care in the world. On the inside, though, I was still learning, still searching for meaning. Oh, I didn't wake up in the mornings and announce that today I would search "for meaning." My quest was not that defined yet. It was still back there inside my subconscious mind. I knew I wanted a better life. I had not yet flushed out what that meant. When I had competed, I had "seen" the jump before every performance. I did not realize at the time that I could use the same technique to "see" what I wanted—in full detail. Oh, I would have flashes of images, but it was far from a concentrated mental and spiritual effort.

I even had a book written about me: *The Perfect Jump: The Rise and Fall of an American Athlete.*

I was so flattered when Dick Schaap, the author, came to San Diego to interview me for his book in 1976. It supposedly spanned the first thirty years of my life. People who read it told me it was not that flattering, but it was certainly not tabloid stuff. I haven't read the book and it has been out of print for years now. Why? I didn't want to see Dick's interpretation of how I lived, so I didn't read it.

After all these years, I still had the notion that anyone who smiled at me had my interest at heart—especially an attractive female. Was I yearning for the mother I had never had? The motives for the kisses, the hugs and the affection somehow got all mixed up in my brain. I wanted to please more than most people do. I wanted to be well liked and to have your attention more than most. Inside, I was still the neglected and abandoned little five-year-old who was invisible.

Early in 1981, ABC Sports invited me down to Miami to participate in their *Superstars* television special. Miami is a beautiful place. I had been down there once before in the 1960s. Gloria had family there who owned a funeral home and I stayed with them while I competed.

So there I was on Key Biscayne, surrounded by blue sky and crystal-clear water. It was February and the weather was breezy and in the mid-seventies and I loved it. Dr. Chuck Penzodlt of the county parks department asked me if I would like to work for him bringing international track meets to Miami. Perfect timing again.

Weeks later, I moved to Miami and leased an apartment in South Miami. We organized major meets for more than two years. The best and brightest of track and field from the United States, South America and the Caribbean would come to compete. Each year the event became better and better.

I worked hard. I continued to travel and speak, mostly to kids, with whom I'd share the trials and tribulations of my childhood. So many little things had inspired me over the years: a word, a smile, a gesture. I hoped that through each of my shared experiences I could leave something with them that might connect with their daily dilemmas.

The meets were yanked from under me; my reward for doing what my boss called a "great job." There had been complaints from narrow-minded promoters who were the constituents of nervous politicians. I was a threat. How does "a New York Bob Beamon" get so much support—and without their help. They would rather destroy the entire concept than share in a larger arena. That narrow thinking was what was wrong with track and field in general, and certainly what was wrong with Miami. That I was able to move so freely in the international track world that I didn't need their sanctions or contacts must have threatened them. I was an Olympic champion who had made a name for himself in that world.

There was a local black promoter who complained that I was getting all the support. There was plenty of room for what he did and for what I was doing. It was on two different levels. But Miami was run like a little one-horse town then. It had the cruise ships, the beaches and the sun, but for a black man, it was still the deep South. In hindsight though, I realize that it was not to the advantage of the local politicians to behave differently. They preferred to attract mediocre talent because on that level they had their greatest control.

Sad to say, blacks and whites still suffered from having that plantation mentality—only one overseer and only one HNIC: head nigger in charge.

My next assignment with the parks department was to maintain the golf course on Key Biscayne, the same golf course at which I had appeared as a celebrity superstar. I took the assignment with a positive attitude. Instead of humiliation, I felt serene, surrounded by rolling greens and blue sky. My work attire changed from suits and ties to shorts and T-shirts.

I kept a low profile for a while. I learned all I could about maintaining a first-class golf course. I developed a camaraderie with the other workers.

I had changed. I became more and more introverted. I was going to work wearing rough-dry shorts and T-shirts and carrying a lunch pail. People in Miami would talk about me as though I was history. "Oh that man used to be an Olympic champion," they would say, pointing at me.

I was gaining weight. I was puffing away on cigarettes, drinking beer and Hennessey cognac. I had married again! I met Georgia at the parks department. She worked as a clerk-typist and had always been helpful to me when I was putting together projects. We became close and started living together.

After the golf-course job, I became the park manager at Gwen Cherry Park, a large park with a pond, located in the middle of Liberty City in Miami's inner-city. There were people that came through the park with all sorts of stories. I threw my energies into the park coming out on top when inspection time came. Across the street were the housing projects; not high-rise ones like in New York but row-house type. The park had been a major meeting place for the local drug dealers. There were people who were always asking for "a little change" and there were people who wanted to clean up the park. Then there were young girls and women who had more babies than they could provide for.

Deanna's mother was one of those women. Deanna's mother, who was a frequent face at the park, struggled to carry a toddler and keep up with her other six children.

When I first laid eyes on Deanna, she looked like a chocolate porcelain doll. And she became the impetus for my marriage to Georgia.

I saw some cigarette burns on Deanna one day, which alarmed me. I knew her mother hadn't burned her but her mother couldn't watch out for her all the time. She had a low-paying job and lots of mouths to feed without help from their fathers. That day I decided to go to her mother's workplace and ask if she'd allow me to take care of Deanna.

"Yes, you can take her because I can't take care of her," she said.

Even though I initiated the situation with Deanna, Georgia wanted Deanna, too. I thought it was only right to marry Georgia once we decided to raise her. Deanna looked like she belonged to me and I loved her as I'd never loved anyone before. It was as if God sent her to me.

I told my friend Sudie Davis that I was going to marry Georgia and the reason why.

"You're kidding me, Bob," he said. "You are kidding me, right? Aw no, man, please don't say 'I do' to her. Bob, I'm telling you, it's not the right situation for you. You'll be sorry."

Sudie Davis was a track coach at Chicago State University when I met him in 1984. We hit it off instantly. Our relationship had become so close, I considered him my brother, cousin and friend. He started coming down to Miami to visit. He knew what I was faced with here. I made a half-hearted effort to leave Miami for Chicago after the track meets were axed, but I never followed through. I wanted stability and I was tired of moving around. I also think the thought of a winter with that whipping Chicago wind, "the almighty hawk," may have influenced me a bit.

Sudie pleaded with me to reconsider the marriage. But I ignored him and my instincts.

He told me I'd be making one of the worst mistakes of my life, but I could not see it at the time. I wanted to have a family. I would do what I had to do to make it work. All I could see was living an altered version of *Ozzie and Harriet*.

* * *

Back in New York, Tim, the youngest son of Bert and Daddy, was serving ten years under the habitual offender act. He had represented himself in court. Lawyers say that a man who represents himself has a fool for a client. Tim was no different. The judge threw the book at him. It broke my heart to see someone with so much talent and potential wasted behind bars. Bert was crushed. Tim was her favorite boy; she'd do everything she could for him.

Chris, the older son, was destined to repeat the Beamon pattern. Damn, I prayed that he would break the vicious cycle. But it was not to be. He'd go into jail and come out of jail. Then he would repeat the cycle all over again. Sad. Really sad.

Nanette, the only girl in the family, managed to become a government employee, mother and wife, but she could not break away from living in the same public housing in which she was raised. I never understood that. She always told me that she was moving—but the moving van never came.

There arc many talented people with potential. But talent has to be combined with discipline, desire and preparation in order to be fulfilled. How many people do you know with raw talent who can draw, sing, cook, write, build? How many do you know who already have an attitude of: "I don't have to learn anymore. You can't tell me nothing, I'm already a star!." Huh? Those are people standing in their own way.

* * *

It was 1986 and I had accepted my reality: I was silly to have such expectations of being loved and in love. I knew I was being punished for all my errors in judgment, lies and mistakes. I resigned myself to living on the surface knowing it would be too painful to penetrate it. I continued to ignore my instincts. It turned out to be a "bad" season for me.

Ma died. She was in her eighties. She had just been brought home from the hospital, and died at home as she wanted, surrounded by her things. Mount Calvary A.M.E. Church was packed with church members, friends and Eastern Stars who came there to send Ma away in style. She had lived a long life, but that was no comfort to me. Although I felt distanced from her since the Melvina fiasco, I loved her no less. Besides Deanna, Ma was all I had.

I went to her burial at Flushing Cemetery. On a headstone not far from her plot, I saw my mother's name: Naomi Brown Beamon—November 21, 1921 - July 31, 1947. Some powerful force seemed to push me to the ground and fling me on top of her grave. I never knew she was buried there. No one had ever told me, and I never asked. Suddenly, she was real to me. *She had really lived.* I could *feel her* when I buried my hands and the side of my face in her soil. I sobbed uncontrollably.

"Mama. Mama! Oh, Mama why did you have to leave me so alone?"

I had been living forty-something years with all that pent-up emotion. My God! My God!

I lost it. I shut down completely. The level of my grief was as though Ma and Mama had died together. I flooded my body with cigarettes, alcohol and junk food. I stopped my half-hearted attempts at working out. Here I was, a so-called champion, attending a banquet, puffing on a cigarette in one hand, and a glass of cola and cognac on the rocks in the other. I looked and acted like a defeated has-been instead of a living legend.

"It was like seeing a gazelle with a cigarette. I mean here was this man, a man who leaped with such grace and beauty, with a body that was sculpted with pure muscle. I finally meet him and he's got a cigarette dangling from his lips. It was difficult to shake that image," remembers Lloyd Morber, M.D.

* * *

It was 1988, I got a call from Nanette. She told me Daddy was in the hospital and very sick and that I needed to come see him. I flew to New York. Nanette had not prepared me for what I saw.

As I walked through the door of his hospital room, a pungent odor hung in the air. I pulled back the curtain and froze. I could not believe my eyes. Daddy's muscular 160-pound frame had wasted away to under one hundred pounds. He was a living skeleton. He recognized me and motioned for me with his eyes to come closer. He struggled to breathe as he spoke. "I want you to know, I never did agree with you getting married to Melvina. That was your grandmother's plan. I never felt good about that. There was something about Melvina that just wasn't right, just wasn't right," he mumbled. "Had to tell you that."

At this point I was numb. Nothing was making sense to me.

"Daddy, I came as soon as Nanette called me. I didn't know you were in the hospital. How're you feeling?"

He ignored my question. His mind was somewhere else.

"Bobby, I want you to have my house upstate. My children wouldn't appreciate it. They've disappointed me so." He choked as he chose each word slowly, carefully. "I'm so proud of you."

Tears poured down my cheeks as I held his bony hand in that room where the odor of death was all around us. Daddy had told me that he was proud of me. He had really turned his life around since he had been with his current wife. He had stopped drinking and had been a shoemaker for the last twenty years. I guess he was trying to make up for all the years of hurt by offering his property to me. It was a house that I had visited only twice. But I did not even consider taking it. It would have created too many problems. I kept his offer to myself.

I left New York. Queens was cursed. Every time I went there I felt zapped of energy and sick. Every time the phone rang and the call was from Queens, my gastric juices would boil. I would always anticipate the worst. Queens—it symbolized the worst that could happen to me.

Daddy died shortly after my visit. I remember his wake so vividly. I took it harder than I thought I would. Despite all the abuse and disappointment, I loved him. But I will never forget when the somber silence was broken by the clinking of metal on metal. I looked back to see his sons, Chris and Tim, handcuffed and ankle-chained, taking mini-steps down the center aisle. Two sheriffs walked alongside them. My heart stopped for a moment. Chris and Tim walked to Daddy's open casket, paused, and then walked out. They both looked like they had been through hell. Their presence under these conditions was a dubious tribute to their father.

What I retained from this relationship was his gold wedding band, wristwatch and pair of woven socks with gold threads that I'd always admired, and many bittersweet memories.

But I had a life to live. The skillet felt safer than the fire, but it all burned. Sudie and I got closer and closer. When I'd go to Chicago I'd stay with him. When he'd come to Miami, he'd stay at my house. My newest challenge was to take a drug-infested park that was a thug hangout in the middle of the inner-city and transform it into a safe clean place for children to play. They had already found a couple of decomposed bodies in the pond.

I threw myself into the task. I developed an inner life like Viktor Frankl, and retreated there. At my house, I'd escape by shutting out the situation. I created a sanctuary inside my headphones where the music blasted so loud in my ears that I was certain to blow out my eardrums. It was simply amazing that the power of the sound did not give me a headache. I guess I was living a headache every day and couldn't tell the difference.

Sudie came down to help me on his vacation. Little by little the riffraff started to disappear from the park. But not without leaving another message. When we were cutting grass, trimming trees and painting, we heard a spray of firepower zip over our heads. We ran for cover, miraculously dodging one bullet after another, and ducked behind a bench. It was scary. Thank God they missed. It was in retaliation for taking their park away from them. When word of what happened got around, people in the neighborhood, fed up with the violence, started coming to the park. They came to classes and meetings, to sit under the trees near the pond—enjoying nature's haven in the midst of man's chaos.

I had another close friend. I met Joey Walker about 1982, when I first arrived in Miami. Then, he was a photographer and a public relations professional for the county government. He was also from up North—Connecticut. He was low-key, but a keen observer. You know the type, a quiet giant, never said much but said plenty. I connected almost instantly to J.W. I could trust him. He liked me for me—not because I was Bob Beamon, the Olympian. I felt comfortable with him; he had a way of keeping me focused when my vision became blurred. He was a no-nonsense kind of guy; the kind who's got your back in times of need. J.W. was and is very special to me.

* * *

I should have been handling my vending machine and toy-store businesses, but I had convinced myself that I was terrible at business. And you know the sad thing about many athletes? We are conditioned to having everything done for us and are rarely hands-on in our own affairs. So, I had developed a life-style of just "showing up" without having participated in the details.

Anybody who claimed to be an agent could represent me, I didn't care. Whoever wanted to help me, could. I didn't ask questions. I didn't ask for references or consider credentials. I figured I'd have nothing to lose. Later, I would find out that some of my representatives had cursed out major corporate clients, double-dipped into the profits of the businesses, and lied about damn-near everything, including their commissions. They "forgot" to pay the rent on a storage space where many of my awards and memorabilia were stored. It was all auctioned off before I even found out about it.

Georgia and I blended like oil and water. We were the subjects of continuous gossip at the parks department—a daily soap opera. I was embarrassed and I was angry with myself. I was making myself sick. I wanted so desperately to walk but I didn't want to disrupt life for Deanna. I wanted to leave the parks department but at least there I was building financial stability. I considered myself stuck.

To many in the sports world I had dropped off the face of the earth. Even people in Miami didn't know I lived there. I had mixed feelings about being visible.

My ears had begun to give me trouble when I traveled by airplane, they would get stopped up from the air pressure. I was scheduled to travel for an appearance and decided to see a doctor to get something for my ears. I weighed in at about 235 pounds. I had a full face and a round gut. I was about eighty pounds heavier than my jumping weight, and fifty pounds heavier than my comfortable weight. When the nurse took my blood pressure, she ran to get the doctor. They sent me directly to the emergency room. My pressure was so high that had I flown on that plane I was sure to have had a heart attack. I came that close.

Something clicked. I had almost died. But someone was watching over me again. I wasn't ready to leave yet. I didn't want to be unhappy anymore.

I began to run again, which put me back in touch with my body. That day in the doctor's office was the last day that I ever smoked a cigarette or took a drink of alcohol, and I completely eliminated pork and red meat from my diet. I began to feel energized. Sudie told me that I needed to stop wearing those 'wrinkled-ass' shorts and shirts and get back to my style and I took his advice.

I left Georgia and found sanctuary in a small apartment. I was doing more and more speaking in the schools. As I told my story, I became inspired by my audiences. I became stronger. I dropped fifty pounds. I regained my energy.

I started playing the congas again. Sudie and I would have this competition over who could compile the most awesome music tape. We shared a love for great music, and Sudie's resemblance to a young Miles Davis was unbelievable. It was weird. He could have been his baby brother.

I was beginning to listen to my instincts. I made a decision: life was too short to be unhappy. I was in my mid-forties and I had never given up in all those years. I never had accepted that we're only allowed to make a certain number of mistakes and then it's over. Who says? Who's making the rules anyway? I decided when it comes to my life, me and God make my rules, and I knew this wasn't the time to be sidelined by mistakes. Everyone makes mistakes. It embarrassed me that I had four failed marriages, but I filed for divorce.

During that process, I looked forward to a very important event—the twenty-fifth anniversary of my Olympic record in 1993. My world record had been broken in 1991 by Mike Powell and he only broke it by two inches. It stood for twenty-three years. But twenty-nine feet two and one-half inches (8.90 meters) was still standing as an Olympic record, the longest in modern-day Olympic history.

It was a major turning point in many ways. People flew in from all over the world. Olympians Lyn Davies came from Great Britain and John Naber from L.A.; Tony Duffy, then president of Allsport; Bud Greenspan, the famed Olympic filmmaker; Dr. Leroy Walker, then president of the United States Olympic Committee; the late Larry Ellis—my high school track coach who coached at Princeton; former Laker James Worthy and so many more. It was a night of kind words and affirmations. I entertained my guests with a drum solo. Grammy winners Betty Wright and Nestor Torres performed a solo and the late Billy Rolle conducted his orchestra. The evening was electric. I soaked in each and every moment.

"He didn't belong there," Coach Ellis told the audience, referring to my experience at the 600 school. "He never belonged there."

Chapter Eleven

Unforgettable

The anniversary celebration was the catalyst that brought us together: She was beautiful, tall, elegant and kind. She was black, a mix of African, Sioux, Cherokee and German. Milana entered my life when she became a member of the committee that organized the event. She owned her own production company and held a Juris Doctorate. She had moved to Miami from Manhattan. But she was born and raised in Chicago.

I met Milana at Vizcaya, the beautiful Mediterranean villa originally built as a winter home by the Deering family in the 1920s, on the edge of Biscayne Bay in Coconut Grove.

I was hosting a reception there for the Atlanta Committee on the Olympic Games (ACOG). Miami was on the short list as a candidate to host the soccer semifinals. Milana had been invited to the reception by my staff and we wanted her to serve on the committee for the anniversary program. She had been recommended to us by Petra Peters, who worked for TV series *Miami Vice* costar Phillip Michael Thomas. Petra knew of Milana's excellent reputation for producing quality work.

She had no idea who I was. She knew I was an Olympian, but that was the extent of it. Although she loved sports, she was more into basketball than track and field. She would tell me later that the one thing that stood out to her about me was my kindness and exquisite manners. She was impressed, she said, with my ease in handling such a diverse crowd.

It was not love at first sight for her or me; but it was certainly mutual admiration. The third time we were together for a dinner meeting, the other people in the restaurant seemed to disappear. We stayed there from seven until midnight—five hours. The next time we had dinner, it lasted for five hours, again. Then we stayed in the parking lot and talked for another hour. Something was definitely happening.

I told her that I had just filed for divorce and that my life was a mess. She told me she had no intention of being involved in any of my confusion! So there was no pressure on me. She was too busy flying off to Paris, New York and Los Angeles— taking care of her own business. I liked that. Milana had her own identity and lived a very interesting life. She wasn't looking to live through me.

In fact, she stopped seeing me. I had too many people pulling at me. In fact, since the word was out I was about to be available, there were suddenly women, some I had known for years, trying to position themselves in my life. Milana didn't want me to want her out of a game of control or a sense of obligation. Milana wanted me to want her because I wanted her. Period.

The night of the anniversary dinner, she wouldn't have anything to do with me. Three weeks earlier, we had this major argument in a restaurant parking lot.

"I have had it up to here with your personal chaos. You don't know if you're coming or going—and I'm not riding on the roller coaster with you. Call me when you get your life together," she said.

She told me I was a spoiled athlete and I didn't know how to treat a woman like her who wasn't a groupie and maybe I needed to get a book to learn how. I was furious with her. How dare she tell me, Bob Beamon, that she was out of my league?

Anyway, she came to the anniversary dinner dressed to kill; made certain the sponsors she brought in and the talent— Grammy winners Nestor Torres and Betty Wright—were taken care of, and then she left! I wondered where she was when she didn't come to the after-party in the Al Capone suite at the Biltmore Hotel.

I had a great time at the after-party. I was singing and being sung to. I couldn't remember when I had more fun. I was humbled by all those who came to celebrate with me. It was another wake-up call!

There were two women there who tried to out-stay each other. So at about dawn, I put everyone out. So there I was in this huge suite, in this huge bed, alone!

A week or so later I received a box sent FedEx from Milana, packed with all the gifts I had given her. The handmade leather mask, signed by a Haitian artist, I had given her for her birthday, the collectible Olympic trading pins, a vintage Alice Coltrane album and more. What kind of woman gives back gifts?

In the attached note she wrote how deceitful I was and that I could never be her man. She never wanted to see me again. Oh, well.

* * *

Now I was an assistant director of Youth Services, a division of the parks department created for me by Chuck Penzoldt. I had been so frustrated, wondering when the department was going to take advantage of my talent and resources. I had been hardworking and dependable for thirteen years.

I designed motivational programs sponsored by the department. We would bring the message of hope to the youth at the schools or in the parks. I was busy making it work by recruiting corporate sponsors to underwrite special events and using my contacts with other athletes to make guest appearances. I was still being contacted every now and then to speak in Europe and out of town.

I told Sudie about Milana. But I was distracted because

Georgia was using every tactic she could to prolong the divorce proceedings. I even broke down in tears once when the judge ordered yet *another* continuance. I was losing my mind. I wanted her out of my life. I wanted to be untangled and free.

Three months had passed since I had seen Milana. Then I saw her with her friend, Jill Tracey, an entertainment reporter, at CoCo Walk. She looked fabulous. Sudie was with me but we had dates with us. I pointed Milana out to him. He tried to catch her as she took the escalator up to the movie theater. I wasn't sure if she had seen me, so I perched myself in eye shot of the movie theater exit in front of Dan Marino's restaurant. I pretended I didn't see her leave and she pretended that she didn't see me waiting. That was in August.

On the afternoon of September 4, 1994, I received a handwritten note on delicate white linen stationery. It read in part: *I hate the way we parted...let's have lunch.*

I didn't hesitate. It was three o'clock. I called her right away. My divorce was final and my head was clearer. My affairs were in order. I was ready for her now. I met her at five, for a late lunch. She told me that when you love someone, sometimes you have to set them free—and if the love was meant to be, then they will fly back to you. I told her that I'd thought she'd never see me again after that first note. I told her I loved her and that I felt we had known each other for years. We have not been apart since that afternoon at Bruzzi's, an Italian restaurant, in Aventura.

* * *

I received a call from the new track coach at UTEP in September 1994. Coach Kitchen invited me to come to El Paso to be entered into their Hall of Fame. I had not been back there since 1969. Milana was looking forward to the experience, and frankly so was I. What struck me most while I was there was that Kitchen seemed to really want to give me "my due" at

UTEP.

Wayne Vandenberg was there. I don't know how long he'd been gone from UTEP, I hadn't seen him in years. He's big in real estate in Chicago, he told me. He looked distinguished dressed in a navy Armani suit.

Coach Kitchen gave me my NCAA championship ring for the long jump and triple jump after twenty-six years had passed. That was special.

A few weeks later, my stepsister, Nanette called me. My stepbrother Tim had died. I knew it was inevitable when I spoke to him some weeks before. He was in the hospital. He was on dialysis. He had AIDS, yet I believe he was still taking drugs. He had only been out of prison for a year. Milana and I flew to New York for his service.

There was no insurance. So Nanette had to have him cremated. This caused controversy because Tim was a Muslim and should not have been cremated. There was no urn, no program. The service was conducted in a storefront church. There were dirty plastic flowers in dirty pink vases sitting on a platform covered by a soiled bedsheet.

Melvina conducted Tim's service. She was some kind of minister now. The tension in that place was so thick you could cut it with a knife. Her words reflected a troubled and bungled lifetime. I found no comfort in Melvina's words, I felt no inspiration, I felt no divinity coming from her. I felt so sad for my brother. There was little compassion in Tim's service. My other stepbrother Chris was there. He was out of jail, married and working as a cook. I was happy for him.

Milana and I felt like we were suffocating, especially after I told her the minister was Melvina. She said she had never been to a funeral that was so negative before. Afterward, we walked the several blocks back to the projects, to get some fresh air.

When we got back to our room at the hotel five minutes from JFK International Airport, the phone rang. It was Toy.

Chris had given her our number. She wanted to get together to "compare notes." I told her "no thanks." All these vultures circling around the prey.

The emotions of Tim's service overwhelmed me. I wept in Milana's arms, she had never seen me like that before. If I could have gotten a flight out at that moment I would have. I wanted to get the hell out of Queens.

My brother Andrew had passed away in 1993. He was fifty. He had spent over forty years in a state institution for the retarded. He had finally found peace.

Milana and I married in late December, 1994. We had an intimate ceremony of family and friends. Milana walked into my arms with baby's breath in her hair and dressed in a turquoise-flowered chiffon dress. She and her dad walked down the aisle to "Unforgettable," sung by Nat King and Natalie Cole. Her brother, Willis Jr., and her sister, Christina Faye, stood by her side. Her mother, Delorese, although unable to make the trip was there in spirit.

Sudie was my best man and J.W. took the pictures. We took our vows in a circle of candles—at the home of friends Ralph and Brenda Williams—illuminated so much like that special cave in Granada, Spain.

Ironically, J.W. knew Milana before I did. He used to sit with her and her dad at the annual county credit union meetings. Her father was a civil engineer with the county.

Less than two months after we married I had been selected to take on a major project that would change my life forever. Milana and I led Arnold Schwarzenegger's Inner-City Games in South Florida for two years. The program reached more than 10,000 children. Through sports and arts, the Inner-City Games exposed our kids to positive alternatives to drugs and violence. It consumed almost every aspect of our lives for those two years.

In the midst of the Games, Milana found out her father was dying from lung cancer. Taking care of him, the pain of watching him suffer, compounded with being at the helm of a high-profile project tested our new marriage to the hilt. I was her rock. I had to be tough with her sometimes to keep her focused. She was slipping—never discomposed, but on edge, impatient and distracted. She was tough, too. Sometimes she was brutal and fragile all at the same time. I hated to see her suffer but I understood having experienced that kind of pain with Daddy and Ma.

We were also working on a television pilot, and we flew to Philadelphia to interview Julius Erving. He granted me permission to conduct the interview in his lovely home, something he had not done before. We had a wonderful conversation, recalling when we first met, his glory days in the NBA and his personal values. This time, Dr. J didn't have to ask me, "Don't you know who you are, Bob Beamon?"

I knew I could fly. I was in an environment that nurtured and encouraged me. My inner fantasy life was no longer necessary. My outer life was full of love.

I was under a press embargo not to reveal that I would participate in the Opening Ceremonies of the Centennial Olympic Games in Atlanta in 1996. Before a worldwide television audience of three billion, I was honored with ten other athletes designated among the greatest Olympians of all times. I walked up to center stage as they called "Bob Beamon—twenty-nine feet two and one-half inches. 1968 Mexico City." I entered the field dressed in a white double-breasted suit, two-toned shoes and waving a white Panama hat. I was so proud to be standing there with my fellow Olympians: Mark Spitz, Greg Louganis, Nadia Comenici and others. When Muhammed Ali lit that Olympic torch, chills ran down my spine. What a moment! What a champion!

There is nothing like the feeling of thousands of people cheering you on. It is indescribable. I was humbled to be in the same company as these champions.

* * *

In the summer of 1995, I left the parks department and started my own business. I did not want to hide out anymore. I wanted to spread my wings and fly.

I had found true love. Our love for each other recognized and nurtured each other's potential, just like Viktor Frankl wrote. With her I have flourished as an artist, designer, musician, advocate for children, professional speaker, businessman, husband and father. I have more confidence in myself. With me she has flourished as a writer, television and film producer/director, fundraiser for children-related charities and as a beloved life companion.

We are talented and strong individuals. Together we are even better.

I have forsaken my quest for an *Ozzie and Harriet* lifestyle—it was a script not written for me. I have found happiness in my own concept of family. Deanna is growing up to be a wonderful human being: compassionate, competitive and accomplished. She is an honor student and raises prizewinning steers for her 4H club. It is something to watch her, petite and tough, manage to control a fourteen hundred pound steer. Although she lives with Georgia, I am and always will be there for her with unconditional love.

It is our responsibility to ourselves to seek and find our own meaning of life, to find love, to fulfill our most deepest desires and to believe that we deserve to be happy. You can get through the rain, the blizzard and the earthquake. If I can do it, you can do it.

See through the cracked glass. Don't be side tracked, and if you are, don't stay there. Get up and move.

It's simple. You never fail until you quit. There is no such thing as three strikes and you're out in the game of life.

Just think about it. Suppose I had quit? Yes, I made mistakes. I fell on my face dozens of times. I made bad choices.

I made great choices. I was naive. I was smart. I refused to stay down.

Lessons are repeated until they are learned.

I was praised in the media. I was humiliated and hurt by the media. I had to live under the double standards of poverty; the economic and psychological disparities of racial prejudice. I lived among people who resented me, people who were celebrity groupies, people who only saw me as their meal ticket or their ticket to a better life, people who drained me—and people who energized me.

When the student is ready the teacher will appear.

I had to rid myself of my own demons. I had to rise above my personal issues of abandonment, abuse and need for attention. I had to be honest with myself and accept the fact that many times I was sending mixed signals: sometimes on purpose, sometimes not. But I kept going until I got it right.

Yes, this is my story. The story of Bob Beamon, a man who didn't want to be anything in particular in the beginning. I have opened up my life to you. Shared my personal business with you. Damn-near stripped naked in front of you. Why? Because I feel we are all here to give something to one another. That we all have our own unique purpose with our own tailor-made lessons. If I had not been inspired by people like Larry Ellis, Ralph Boston, Viktor Frankl, Martin Luther King, Jr., John F. Kennedy, Mrs. Manchuca, Mrs. Kiska and so many others, where would I be now? Maybe you will find something in my words that will inspire you. I hope that each and every day I will continue to find inspiration in living and giving.

I am the man who could fly—and I am still flying. God bless.